Praise for 'Women on Fire, Volume 2'

"Looking for inspiration? Look no further than Debbie Phillips and these stories from Women on Fire. Wow!"
> ~ **Judy Blume,** best-selling author, *Are You There God? It's Me, Margaret, Summer Sisters, Starring Sally J. Friedman as Herself* and many more

"I applaud the incredible courage it took for each of these women to share their life experiences in this wonderful collection of stories. As I read them, I got chills! I was captivated, motivated and inspired."
> ~ **Nancy Kramer,** founder and CEO, Resource, named by *Advertising Age* as one of the 100 most influential women in the history of advertising

"With her rare ability to observe sensitive and enriching moments in people's lives and treat their stories with care and love, Debbie Phillips has created a special way for women from all walks of life to write about their unique and universal experiences. See for yourself and enjoy this book. It's a keeper."
> ~ **Ann Graham,** business journalist

"If you've never had the electrifying pleasure of attending a Women on Fire tea, put the kettle on the stove and get ready to curl up with this magnificent book. You'll particularly need that hot tea because this is a compilation of stories bound to give you chills. Twenty-one remarkable women serve up their souls, their hearts, and their wisdom with a warmth and honesty that

makes you feel like you just shared a group hug. I loved it. The only part missing is the scones."

~ **Linda Yellin,** author, *The Last Blind Date*
and *What Nora Knew*

————

"Women on Fire is powered by storytelling—stories that spark transformations, heal our hearts, ignite our imaginations, steel our wills, and drive us to action. This book is a wonderful collection of such stories. Inspiring!"

~ **Noelle Celeste,** publisher of *Edible Cleveland*
and owner of Branching Out, a consulting practice
for innovative businesses and non-profits

————

"After meeting Debbie Phillips and becoming a member of Women on Fire, my life changed and my career exploded! Having guidance and mentorship from Debbie helped me strategically plan out how to build exactly what I had been seeking. She saw my vision and held space for it to manifest, even if I became overwhelmed or discouraged.

My Women on Fire sisters are there to encourage, brainstorm, listen and cheer me on, as my wildest dreams become my reality. If you have been looking for an awesome tribe of conscious, successful, caring women look no more, Women on Fire is it!"

~ **Terri Cole,** licensed psychotherapist,
transformation coach, founder and CEO,
Live Fearless and Free

————

"In a world where women make up half of the humans on earth, 'human rights' often means rights for people of the male gender, with the rights of the other gender lagging far behind.

Debbie Phillips, the visionary force of Women on Fire, is doing important work. Empowering individual women and sharing their stories propels action. Action propels change. Women on Fire is a force for change and a force for good for both genders."
~ **Wendy Taucher,** director, choreographer, author, and artistic director of Wendy Taucher Dance Opera Theater and World Choreography Institute

---

"Looking for a can't-miss investment? Set aside some of your valuable time to read this book and watch the magic begin to unfold in your life. Through the tales of 21 remarkable women you will be swept away by the experience of love, loss, success, and struggle that are the raw and powerful ingredients of becoming your authentic self and finding the work you were meant to do. Debbie Phillips has done it again—it is impossible to read Women on Fire, Volume 2 *and not come away the richer for it."*
~ **Manisha Thakor,** founder and CEO, MoneyZen Wealth Management, and co-author of *Get Financially Naked* and *On My Own Two Feet*

Praise for 'Women on Fire, Volume 1'
Winner of the
2010 National Indie Excellence Book Award

"Margaret Mead once said, 'Never doubt that a small group of thoughtful, committed citizens can change the world ... it is the only thing that ever has.' And I would add, 'especially a group of women.' Women are a powerful lot. We are the creators of change. And when we get to work, we make great things happen. Thank you, Debbie, for creating a venue where women can gather to make great things happen, not only in their own lives, but in the lives of others."

> ~ **Jennifer M. Granholm,**
> former governor of Michigan

"Where was this book 30 years ago when I was starting out? A welcome reminder that you gain more from adversity and failure than success!"

> ~ **Erin Moriarty,** CBS News correspondent

"This book is an inspiring, motivating treasure of women's triumphs over their challenges. It is destined to be placed on every woman's bookshelf right between Chicken Soup for the Woman's Soul and Eat, Pray, Love."

> ~ **Dr. Ranjana Pathak,** corporate vice president
> and creator of www.ombics.com

"Debbie Phillips' inner flame burns so brightly that all who surround her are caught up in the conflagration. In Women on

Fire *she has assembled a luminous group to tell their inspiring stories, ones that move us and challenge us to reach farther than we thought possible.* Women on Fire *is testimony that, if we continue to nurture the inner spark, it cannot help but ignite powerful transformation. Debbie is a nurturer of sparks. She should be forced to wear a sign that says, 'DANGER: HIGHLY EXPLOSIVE HERE.'"*

~ **Edward L. Beck,** CNN News contributor
and author of *Soul Provider:*
Spiritual Steps to Limitless Love

"This book answers the need of women everywhere who seek the empowerment and support Debbie Phillips so graciously creates as she tends the embers of the heart with such love and skill at her Women on Fire gatherings. Every woman, whether leader, entrepreneur, social activist, partner or mother will join this ever-expanding circle and be immediately enriched in making her own dreams come true."

~ **Ellen Wingard,** executive coach,
chairwoman of World Pulse, and co-author of
Enlightened Power: How Women Are
Transforming the Practice of Leadership

"You deserve to be a Woman on Fire in your life. You deserve to read this delicious gem of a book, in which real women share how they left behind ordinary lives for lives of courage, fun, magic, and true success. You'll find a dynamic support group in these pages!"

~ **Tama J. Kieves,** best-selling author of
Inspired and Unstoppable:
Wildly Succeeding in Your Life's Work

"I have written that women are given poor advice when they are told to join an all-women network. And there's research to show women are more backstabbing to other women than to men. So it's great to see that Debbie Phillips is tackling the problem head-on by creating Women on Fire and environments where women can connect in positive, productive and useful ways. It's about time."

~ **Penelope Trunk,** entrepreneur, blogger,
and author of *Brazen Careerist:
The New Rules for Success*

"At the heart of authentic female wisdom are the values of collaboration, support, and generosity. When these attributes are present, true community and inspired leadership follow naturally. Women on Fire *and its author Debbie Phillips are both the living embodiment of this ancient wisdom that we so urgently need in these difficult times.*

As I read this book, I felt like I was sitting in a circle of wise women warmed and emboldened by the fire of their passion, highest aspiration, and courageous action. With its lively style, fearless stories, and mandate to live your dreams no matter what, Women on Fire *is the perfect antidote in our gloomy and disempowered climate."*

~ **Gail Straub,** co-founder, The Empowerment
Institute and author of *Returning to My Mother's
House: Taking Back the Wisdom of the Feminine*

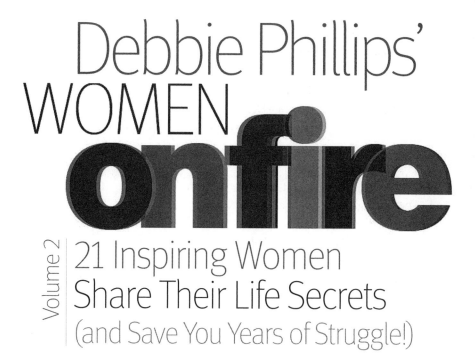

Debbie Phillips'
WOMEN on fire

Volume 2 | 21 Inspiring Women
Share Their Life Secrets
(and Save You Years of Struggle!)

WOMEN on fire MEDIA

WEST TISBURY, MA

Published by Women on Fire Media
West Tisbury, MA
www.womenonfire.com

ISBN: 978-0-9893676-0-8

Cover design, layout, and typesetting: Sebastian Kaupert
Publisher: Sophfronia Scott
Editor: Kacy Cook
Cover photo: Peter Hurley

Printed in the United States of America

For you…
wherever you may be on your journey

In memory of Jane Juergens
She is gone from our sight, but her light still shines

TABLE OF CONTENTS

FOREWORD BY AGAPI STASSINOPOULOS   XIII

INTRODUCTION   XV

PART ONE: INSPIRATION

LAYING DOWN ROOTS IN A NEW LAND   3
Young immigrant, with only $200 and an open heart, transforms her life
Heike M. Vogel

NEVER TOO YOUNG, NEVER TOO OLD   13
Always learning, always growing, always fulfilled
Marge Snyder

ONE IN A MILLION   23
Reconnecting with a child given up for adoption
Mary Kay Purdy

ADOPTION: A RELATIVE COMEDY   33
Re-defining my existence after meeting my biological mother
Sarah Elizabeth Greer

A NEW KIND OF NORMAL   45
A daughter fights for her family when their world is turned upside down
Kim Davis

I'M MARRYING ME   55
Getting unstuck for the sake of living authentically
Beth (Kloesener) Bryce

PART TWO: STRATEGIES

PUSHED BACK TO SQUARE ONE   69
Re-building a life, block by block
Leah Hamilton

SCALING NEW HEIGHTS   79
A mother conquers her phobia to become a better parent
Carrie Saba

HIS, HERS, AND OURS   89
Successful co-parenting by design
Maria Verroye

WILL NO ONE HELP ME?   99
Advocating for my ADHD child in a system that doesn't understand
Susan Kruger

LIFE ALONG THE BORDERLINE   109
Confronting my daughter's mental illness
Kay Raypholtz

FROM SHAME TO FREEDOM   119
The unexpected gifts of an eating disorder
Laurel Hodory

GETTING OFF THE BIPOLAR ROLLER COASTER   131
Stepping onto solid ground after learning to stop the ride
Nicole Friedler Brisson

TAKING CONTROL OF MY FEARFUL LIFE   141
Step-by-step strategies lead from panic attacks to confidence
Mary Carran Webster

PART THREE: SUPPORT

THROUGH THE FIRE   155
One woman's story of addiction and recovery
Jenifer Madson

VOICE LESSONS   165
Learning to speak up for myself and others
Linda Neff

TOUCHED BY SUICIDE   177
A sister's journey of grief, guilt, and shame
Tricia Simpson

WHAT'S IMPORTANT NOW   187
An unexpected caregiver role brings perspective and strength
Marilyn Brown

GETTING BACK TO LIFE   197
Persevering through a mother's catastrophic injuries and illness
Michelle Whittaker

LEANING INTO GRIEF   207
Feeling my way toward healing
Lisa Umberger Arundale

FINDING MY NEXT   217
How I decided what to do with the third third of my life
Jan Allen

PHOTO OF AUTHORS OF *WOMEN ON FIRE, VOLUME 2*   226

ACKNOWLEDGMENTS   227

20 ASPIRATIONS OF WOMEN ON FIRE   232

AN INVITATION FROM DEBBIE   234

ABOUT DEBBIE PHILLIPS   236

CONTACT   239

FOREWORD

I was born in Greece, but I was educated and lived in England, where teatime is a great daily ritual—a happy hour! Over a cup of tea, you bond, relax, chat, and recharge.

What stands out most from my first Women on Fire tea—in New York City in 2004—is a warm feeling of connection and oneness. There was an intimacy and safety in the women sharing with each other, even though many of them had just met for the first time. Everyone around the table was heard and included. When I look at photographs from that day, I still feel the joy that was radiating out.

Women on Fire is a community of women who come together to really support each other and ensure that whatever the need is—whether it relates to work or career or a personal longing—each woman can be heard, inspired, understood, and supported.

In a most powerful and natural way, this fellowship provides a space for women to break through. We all want our "next thing," but along the way we might realize that it is not a "thing" at all that we seek, but rather a greater sense of self and feelings of belonging and fulfillment.

And the way to get there is through what I call an "unbinding of the heart." By letting someone into your heart, as we do in

Women on Fire, you allow her to come out to be her true self, to feel safe in the world. This unbinding happens through caring, listening, and extending our hearts to reach one another. Women on Fire are like that; they jump in to support each other with love and compassion. It is an alive, empowering, nurturing community that comes together over tea and empathy.

From the first time I met Women on Fire Founder Debbie Phillips, I saw how she herself exuded this generosity, always asking, "How can I support you? How can we be together? How can I make you part of my life and help you succeed?" She is the open gate to a gorgeous garden, beckoning you, "Come in! Come in! You are all the beautiful flowers of the world! Come in and join the other beautiful flowers!"

Following Debbie's example, the women I meet at Women on Fire are extremely generous, kind, open, and fun. They have the ability to make a place in their lives for other women. They open the door to possibilities for women that go beyond any labels—you're young, you're old, you're successful, you're stuck, you've gone through a failure, you're newly married, you're newly divorced, you're looking for a relationship. None of that matters! There is no hierarchy, but a sense of sameness that bridges the illusion of separation.

This rich volume of stories is everything Women on Fire stands for. It is a heart-opening work that will be your Woman on Fire companion in print.

Whatever is in your heart to open up to next, we are here at Women on Fire to support you. Let's do it together. Let me light your fire … while you ignite mine. We've got each other's hearts.

Agapi Stassinopoulos
Author, *Unbinding the Heart: A Dose of Greek Wisdom, Generosity, and Unconditional Love*

INTRODUCTION

You have in your hands (or at your fingertips!) the second volume of our Women on Fire book series. The enormous response to the first one, our award-winning *Women on Fire: 20 Inspiring Women Share Their Life Secrets (and Save You Years of Struggle!),* made it clear that there is a powerful need for women to reach out to each other to share their real-life challenges and solutions.

So we have returned with even more stories from courageous women who reveal their deepest secrets, their wounds and battles, so that you can see how they navigated, survived, and eventually triumphed. The authors generously lay bare their hearts and histories to provide comfort, clarity, encouragement, and sisterhood to reassure you along your own path.

Each chapter is an individual woman's journey—the challenges she faced and the insights, strategies, and support she used to move through and beyond her most difficult times. You may recognize yourself in a story, or in parts of many, or in all of them. Because the authors are women like you. Their struggles and situations could have pulled them under. But no matter how tough the circumstances, they never stopped in their quests to learn, to grow, and to find a better place.

This book is only one of many ways to connect with the

Women on Fire community. Women on Fire was created to bring women together to support one another, to expand the opportunities for women to live their dreams, and to foster a world where women achieve success on their own terms.

Since the publication of the first Women on Fire book four years ago, I've received an avalanche of emails and letters from readers who were deeply touched, comforted, and motivated to move their own lives forward. I have every reason to believe you will love and be inspired by these stories just as much!

Debbie Phillips
Martha's Vineyard, Massachusetts

PART ONE: INSPIRATION

LAYING DOWN ROOTS IN A NEW LAND

*Young immigrant, with only $200
and an open heart, transforms her life*

Heike M. Vogel

"The most important decision we make is whether we believe in a friendly or hostile universe." **–Albert Einstein**

How did a German girl, marked to fail, become a successful corporate attorney in New York City—by herself, in a foreign country, without family, money, green card, or mastery of English?

The answer may be surprising. It is not only that my childhood began with sharp contrasts—kindness and violence, joy and sorrow, protection and attack—but more importantly, I learned early on that, when faced with such choices, embracing the gentler, kinder way is more powerful, even if fear is the driving force. But I am getting ahead of myself. Let me go back to my humble beginnings.

I grew up in a small town in Germany, and by small, I mean a population of about 500. It is a beautiful, charming village where everyone knows everyone else. My mother taught me the importance of being polite and greeting the people we met along our walks through town. So I did, cheerfully calling out "Grüß Gott" ("Greet God") to everyone we saw. Needless to say, I was a bit confused when Mom first took me to the nearby city. Although barely able to keep up with them all, I was yelling "Grüß Gott" to every person on the street. Mom explained that the big city, filled with strangers, was not the place to be quite so friendly. It was not easy for me to reduce my greetings from everyone to no one.

But I was a quick study, even at five years old. I had to be. Mom simply did not have the time to watch over me constantly. She worked as a waitress, mostly as an escape from the frightening realities going on inside our lovely home, aptly located across from the village cemetery.

Fortunately, I was not alone. I grew up with two brothers, Burschy and Werner, and a sister, Marion. Burschy, two and a half years older than me, taught me how to tell time, or at least how to follow his instructions regarding time. Before he left the house to catch the school bus, he'd sit me in front of an alarm clock and say, "When the big hand is on 10 and this little hand is on 8, walk to the village deli, buy your lunch biscuit, and then continue to kindergarten." He also tried, not very successfully, to teach me how to defend myself by offering me to let me hit him like a boy.

Marion, who is six years older than me, graciously accepted the role of our caretaker. When she was only a teenager, she made the family dinners and tried her best to be in charge of us. Because of her beauty, our father kept her under close watch. She grabbed the first chance she had to get out by marrying at 18. Several years earlier, Werner, the oldest of our little gang, had joined the German Navy, also at age 18. Indeed, I hardly remember Werner participating in any of our family gatherings, as he had left home when I was barely 4.

Why the exodus, you wonder? Allow me to introduce our father, the raging alcoholic.

At his office, our father was respected as a hard-working, reliable, intelligent, charming, and generous man. And he was generous—with the outside world. Who would suspect that the caviar and expensive delicatessens he purchased were for his own consumption, while the rest of us ate only the salami Mom bought at the supermarket?

He also was very reliable. He never missed a day of work or arrived late, regardless of what might have occurred at home the night before. As Mom would point out, our father was not like the village drunk who couldn't hold on to a job and lost all sense of shame by being openly inebriated in broad daylight. He made it to the office, appearing stone sober, even after a drunken rage throughout the night, wearing an impeccable suit and standing proudly at his full six feet three inches tall.

Dad drove a Mercedes, and we were keenly aware of the sound of its engine. As soon as one of us would yell, "Listen! Dad's car!" we'd all jump into action. Lights out! Pretend to be asleep! I learned to pray, "Dear God, please just make him fall asleep on the couch." When this prayer wasn't answered and the shouting began, I prayed, "Dear God, please don't let him hurt Mom."

I was mostly spared from being an eyewitness to his violent outbursts. But one incident remains etched in my memory: I could not have been much older than 4. Marion, when I talked to her about it years later, had hoped that I had been too young to recall. But I can still see Marion, Burschy, and me standing in the door to our parents' bedroom, holding hands as we watched our father strangling our mother, his big hands wrapped tightly around her throat, his tall physique pushing down on her small body. Only five minutes earlier, Mom was getting dressed, her pretty green eyes gazing lovingly at me, her freshly tinted lips smiling. And then this scene—her mouth gasping for air, her eyes filled with fear, not so much of death, but more for us standing there, watching. Perhaps it was the sight of us, or maybe it was the threat of imprisonment that made him let go of her. Of course, our house was not always the backdrop of a possible murder scene. We also had fun and learned not to take things too seriously. Mom often reminded us that we had a choice in every situation: we could either laugh or cry. She always suggested laughter.

As the youngest, I was doted on by my siblings. I was lovingly referred to as "Kleene," or "Little One." Werner, the oldest, was generous and laid back. Even though our father hurled the harshest insults at him, Werner never retaliated because Mom pleaded with us to never talk back to our father, which she said only made things worse. To help keep the peace, Werner mostly stayed away, visiting only when our father wasn't home.

Burschy was tall, soulful, and popular. Being an animal lover, he constantly brought home the oddest rescues. Among other strays he nurtured back to health were a crow, Hansi, and a buzzard, Dora. Burschy didn't believe in caging animals, so Hansi nested in the walnut tree in our garden, but preferred hanging out inside our house, searching for anything sparkly. Several times, Burschy had to climb up to Hansi's nest to retrieve a neighbor's spoon or button that Hansi had snatched from an open window. Dora liked to sit on the roof of our uncle's barn across from our house. When Hansi and Dora crossed paths, a scene would erupt, and Mom had to scold and separate them. But Burschy needed only call their names, and the little troublemakers would land on his outstretched arm.

One summer evening, while I was playing at a friend's house, our father, under the influence and in anger, lured trusting Hansi to him and, before Burschy's eyes, snapped Hansi's little neck. Burschy went to his room sobbing, but composed himself so he could gently give me the sad news. I remember his smiling face when he came to my friend's house, declaring it was time for him to walk me home. He put his arm around me and explained that Hansi was now in heaven. He assured me that even though it would be quiet without our little rascal, he was not sad, knowing that Hansi was high up in the sky. He did not lie about the terrible cause of Hansi's death, but he did conceal his grief to help me overcome mine.

As hard as he may have tried, our father could not snuff out Burschy's kindness, joy, or humor. Burschy shielded me from our father's violent outbursts. He once warned that if Dad should as much as break a hair on Little One's head, he would have to answer for it. Burschy's shield was not just physical; it included his belief in and encouragement of me. When our father would tell me that I'd always be a failure, Burschy loudly whispered, "You mean everything to me; you can do anything." How could I not believe him—my hero, protector, friend, and big brother?

When I was 15, Burschy was killed in a car accident. A few days later, he appeared to me in a dream. He floated above the living room door looking confused, sad, and lost. He asked me, "Why can I not be with you?" For three years, I asked that same question. I was left alone with our mother and father and didn't have the strength to protect her or myself. So I went inside, literally and figuratively. I left the house only to go to school and otherwise stayed in my room, sleeping, crying, studying, and staring into space. Did I live in a friendly or hostile universe?

ESCAPE FROM MADNESS

At first Burschy's death brought some peace to our house. There were times of stillness, but our father's insane outbursts continued. During one particularly bad evening, Werner, for the first time, stood up to protect me. I didn't hesitate when he instructed me to pack my things to move in with him. On the way out, we ran into Mom and took her too. For months our father did not know where she was. Those were happy, peaceful times. Then Dad found her and she returned to him. It felt like a betrayal; the possibility of a normal future faded.

As hostile as the universe may have felt, friendliness still found its way to me. A teacher, recognizing the state I was in, suggested that, after my graduation, I become an au pair to a nice family in New York City, caring for their two-year-old daughter. An entire year of peace! I first thought the noise of the big city would drive me crazy, but it was there that I found my sanity.

After being away and at peace for an entire year, the hostility I had been accustomed to all my life now seemed so much more hostile. I had to act quickly before I would get used to it again. In less than six months, I used my savings for an airplane ticket back to the United States. I was supposed to stay for just two weeks, so I had only one suitcase and $200. But at the end of my vacation, I simply didn't leave. I called my parents and told them not to drive to the airport in Frankfurt, because I would not be on the airplane. Mom was sad, but she knew this would save me. I didn't call anyone else out of fear that the longing for Marion, Werner, and my German friends might make me go back. It was December 1983, and I was barely 19 years old.

But I didn't have time to feel lonely, and the kind people of the small community on Long Island embraced me. For more than three years, I worked seven days a week. My first job was at a Pancake Cottage as a bus girl, clearing tables and refilling coffee cups. My language skills weren't fluent enough to be a waitress.

I taught myself English, opened a bank account, and got my driver's license, but U.S. immigration laws offered few options for me to qualify as a legal alien. Enter John, who often came to the restaurant where I now waitressed, no longer just a bus girl. He owned a landscaping company and hired me to work days when I wasn't waitressing. He further discovered that his business qualified under a new law that allowed people who worked on farms to apply for a green card. He offered to sponsor me. Finally, after five years of filling out applications and appearing before immigration authorities, I became a permanent U.S. resident.

In 1991, it was time for my next goal: college. I visited several schools before arriving at Columbia University. I immediately knew I had to study there. It was the only place where I applied. To my delight, I wasn't merely accepted—I was offered a merit scholarship. It covered 50 percent of my tuition, although it required me to maintain a 3.33 grade point average. Then my self-studies paid off; I scored so well on the test of English as a Foreign Language that Columbia's administration suggested I enroll as a native speaker instead of a foreign student. Still, I constantly fought my father's voice in my head: "You don't have what it takes. You can't do it." With tears rolling down my face, I'd argue back: "Yes, I can." And I did. In 1995, I graduated cum laude.

I had taken a class in constitutional law and was drawn to law's approach of solving issues. The study of law offers a way to defend others or oneself with reason, not force; the brain is indeed more powerful and resilient than fists. Even though the law needs to be consistent, it is not stale; it slowly evolves to consider ever-changing situations.

After working for over a year as a legal secretary to earn money for tuition, I started at Brooklyn Law School in 1997. On the first day, Victoria Bach, a Russian woman my age, sat next to me. For the next three years, she and I not only took the same classes we also studied together afterward. Studying with Victoria helped ease the intense demands of law school. When weariness would set in, we'd make each other laugh or encourage each other to keep going.

Although law school introduces different legal areas, after the first year, students are expected to narrow their particular area of practice, which was disappointing to me because I liked the variety. Then, in my second year, I became the student law clerk of a New York bankruptcy judge. I learned that bankruptcy law actually encompasses diverse areas and includes transactional as well as litigation matters. It requires an understanding of business as well as human nature as there can be so much at stake when companies are at the brink of closing their doors or when individuals find themselves in economic despair. At its core, bankruptcy law is not about winning or losing; it is about finding solutions that will benefit all parties.

My introduction to bankruptcy law led me to the great honor of becoming law clerk to the brilliant Honorable Richard L. Bohanon. Judge Bohanon would become not only my teacher but also my mentor and adviser for more than 10 years. He treated me like a daughter, allowing me to experience having a loving, supportive father. When I received offers to work at several large law firms, Judge Bohanon counseled me during my years as an associate at "big law." He took every opportunity to tell me how proud he was of me.

Victoria and I not only studied during law school, we also became inseparable during six weeks of nonstop studying for the New York bar exam, and just for good measure, we tossed in the New Jersey bar exam as well. Our hard work paid off when we each passed both bar exams on the first try.

LEARNING FORGIVENESS

Seven years after I moved to the United States, Mom died at the age of 56. She had been sick for more than a year. I hadn't been home for five years when I returned to visit her in the hospital. She no longer recognized anyone. As I sat by her bed, she silently stared up at the sky through the window behind her. She passed away the day before Burschy's birthday. At my graduation from Columbia, only my roommate and two friends attended, but I believe that two more people were present, watching over me and beaming with pride. For my law school graduation, Marion, Werner, two cousins, and an aunt traveled from Germany to celebrate with me.

I tried for a time to reconcile with my father, but he soon remarried and moved away. After almost 10 years without any contact, Marion reconnected with our father when she ran into him in a hospital where his wife was receiving chemotherapy. Marion, a nurse and ever caring for others, could not help but be there for him. Werner and I supported Marion's decision to reconnect, but we preferred to keep our distance.

Marion was with our father when he died. She told me that even up to his final breath, he could not believe that I was an attorney. When she showed him pictures of my law school graduation, he argued that surely I must have graduated as a paralegal and not an attorney.

It took me years to truly understand the meaning of forgiveness. I knew its importance, but first had to learn the difference between forgiveness and indifference. I did on the day I finally felt true compassion for our father. I saw that his insecurities and fears kept him from enjoying and appreciating life. His tremendous self-loathing kept him from receiving the love, kindness, joy, and courage that surrounded him. What unspeakable loneliness and sadness dominated his life? While Burschy, Marion, Werner, and I had each other, banding together against his rage, he had only his self-hatred. And it has been my father's harsh voice that gave me the determination to become who I am today. I am grateful to my father for giving what he could give.

Losing Burschy was the start of my journey within. When the outside world no longer made any sense, the only place left to go was inside. For three years, I was surrounded by darkness; yet during that time, my inner strength began to emerge. Just when I thought life's meaning had been taken away from me, I actually discovered it. Burschy continued to appear in my dreams. I would be overcome with joy as I asked him in disbelief, "You are here with me?" He responded, always smiling, "Of course, where else would I be?" He is, indeed, always with me.

Six years ago, Werner had a massive heart attack. I happened to be in Germany for a wedding just three days earlier. Werner drove for four hours to our little village to spend a brief time with me. I got to hug him and tell him how much I loved him. I was back in New York when Marion called to give me the sad news of his death. Werner taught me the importance of spending time with each other. He used to call me every weekend. Prior to his death, I did not visit Germany often, and I was so glad that I was there then. I now visit often. During Hurricane Sandy, Marion skyped me to keep me company the entire day and night until the storm passed. As we learned as children, together we can face anything.

After more than 10 years of practicing law in large corporate law firms, I've started an exciting venture with my dear friend, Victoria. She is yet another angel sent to walk with me on this incredible journey. We have founded our own firm, VOGEL BACH, P.C. Victoria has litigated big, complex cases in various areas of the law. Her broad litigation expertise combines well with my corporate restructuring and bankruptcy law experience. We share the same determination, and outlook on life. Despite perhaps some evidence to the contrary, we believe that we live in a friendly universe. At times it may be hiding, covered entirely by darkness, but friendliness, not hostility, is indeed the driving force.

Heike M. Vogel, Esq., lives in New York City. She is the founder of VOGEL BACH, a law firm that works closely with its clients to find the most beneficial and affordable solutions to any legal situation. Heike and her law partner speak their clients' language—not just plain English but also German and Russian. With her expertise in corporate restructuring, bankruptcy, and business transactions, Heike enjoys counseling entrepreneurs. She especially enjoys putting her clients at ease, shedding light on legal matters that can appear daunting. Heike can be reached at hvogel@vogelbachpc.com or her company website www.vogelbachpc.com.

NEVER TOO YOUNG, NEVER TOO OLD

Always learning, always growing, always fulfilled

Marge Snyder

I remember as if it were yesterday. I was 17 and about to graduate from high school, taking a class called Office Practices. The teacher had to step out and asked me to supervise until she returned. At the end of the period, she thanked me for my help and then said, "I do hope you are planning to go to college."

Until that moment, college was one of the last things on my mind. I had been working after school, Monday through Friday from 5 to 10 p.m., at a lingerie sewing company (read: sweatshop) for 50 cents an hour, with all of my earnings going into our household budget. The only dream I could conjure up was landing a job at Bethlehem Steel Co., where I could use my typing, shorthand, and oh yes, office practices. My teacher could not have realized that her simple comment had planted a seed: College became my ambition. And I could not have realized that it would take me nearly 40 years to reap the bounty sown that day.

I was born in January 1930, delivered by midwife in a house

in Freemansburg, Pa., where my mother and father were living with his parents. Within three years of my birth, that same house would see three deaths—my father, grandfather, and aunt. Tuberculosis, the dreaded disease of that time, claimed them all.

Times were tough, and convenient solutions were appealing. After my mother and her brother-in-law both lost their spouses, they decided to marry each other. They moved in with his parents in nearby Hellertown. There, I began my education in a public school kindergarten. But the following January, we moved to Bethlehem, Pa., where my mother enrolled me mid-term in a Catholic parish school. The Mother Superior was reluctant to place me in the first grade because I had just turned six, but she asked me to read aloud, and I passed her test.

Bethlehem, like so many steel communities in Pennsylvania at that time, had many European immigrants. Hungarian, Polish, German, and Slovakian neighborhoods were common. Hungarian was spoken in our home, and I went to St. John Capistrano Hungarian School, where the pastor taught Hungarian grammar to the eighth-graders. A highlight from my years at the school was being chosen for the lead role in a play performed in Hungarian. I was St. Elizabeth! This brought me the additional "honor" of copying my lines by hand, in Hungarian, into a notebook and then memorizing them. All of my uncles and aunts attended my debut, and I enjoyed my moment of attention. I trace my enduring love of live theater to that play.

MAKING THE GRADE

I went to Liberty High School, where students had to choose a course of study to follow: The academic curriculum was for those who planned to go to college; the commercial curriculum was for those who did not. This was not really a decision for me; I was already in the workforce, spending evenings in the lingerie factory. I followed the commercial curriculum.

My mother got me the job as an embroidery sewing machine operator because she and three of my aunts worked at the factory. I was only 15 when I started, so I needed a government permit. The job was to insert a wooden hoop holding the top of a woman's slip, with stenciled scallops less than a half-inch wide, under the needle, and then sew a specified number of stitches into each scallop. It took three months to master the task; while I was learning, the pay was only 35 cents an hour.

It was common for a needle to penetrate an operator's finger, and I still remember when it happened to me—it was so painful and I was scared. Plus, my mother was my supervisor, and she was a perfectionist. I often thought she expected too much from me. But I also remember that my mother and I developed a closeness during those years, because at the end of each shift, we had a half-hour walk home together.

Most days, I was able to get my homework finished before my shift started, and I was a good student, so I maintained excellent grades. I especially remember an advanced English class. I was the only student in that class enrolled in the commercial curriculum. The teacher was kind and looked out for me. She asked me to be typist for our yearbook.

I was the first in my family to graduate from high school, but because my relatives seemed unaware of the significance, no one came to the ceremony. I had to take a city bus to attend. But when I opened the event program, I saw that I was named the outstanding commercial student! It was a huge surprise.

I applied for a job at Bethlehem Steel Co. and was hired into the typing pool—20 women on electric typewriters with counters recording the number of strokes typed each day. We were Dictaphone transcribers. The room didn't have air conditioning and was very uncomfortable. I was determined to move out of that job. Some of the executives didn't want to use the newfangled

Dictaphones, so they'd request a stenographer. I could take short-hand, so I always volunteered. The legal department started asking specifically for me and then they offered me a job. My three wonderful bosses were my introduction to educated men. I was happy to go to work each day.

With some friends from work, I joined a YWCA organization for young businesswomen. The first big event was a Sadie Hawkins Day dance, where the girls invite the boys. All of us were interested in meeting guys from Lehigh University, the private, elite men's engineering college in Bethlehem. We posted invitations on bulletin boards and at local eateries. Snow was falling on our big night, but we had a good turnout. At one point, all the girls put one of their shoes in the middle of the dance floor and, when the music stopped, the guys were to retrieve a shoe and find its owner. My shoe was the last to be retrieved! Finally, this shy, skinny guy came up to me, and I asked, "What took you so long?" He said he didn't want to get in the middle of all the big football types diving into the pile of shoes. I thought, "This is a smart guy!"

Kent asked to take me home and we started dating. While his family was not wealthy, they saved enough to send their first-born son to a private college. He didn't have extra spending money, so our dates consisted of a lot of walks and 50-cent movies. We also went to lots of "big band" proms at the university. I made all my own formal gowns.

MARRIAGE AND MOTHERHOOD

When I turned 21, Kent asked me to marry him and gave me a beautiful diamond ring. We married before the start of his senior year. He had a summer drafting job that paid for his final year's tuition; I continued my job at Bethlehem Steel, and we planned to live on my earnings. His degree was worth any sacrifice to us, and it laid the foundation for our lifelong commitment to education.

I got pregnant two months after our marriage. The rules at Bethlehem Steel were that a woman had to stop working when her pregnancy showed, so I had to quit my wonderful job when I was four months pregnant. We survived because I got a big typing job for one of Kent's professors. Plus, Kent did all kinds of odd jobs—setting up pins at a bowling alley, selling magazines door-to-door, yard work. He got his bachelor's degree in mechanical engineering, and then soon after, a job in New Jersey. We had such meager funds that we rode to our new apartment in the moving van that was hauling our few possessions.

We also celebrated Kent's graduation with the birth of our first daughter, Kathi. Within a year, her brother Ed was born.

One of my memories from this time was that I looked forward to putting the two babies down for their afternoon naps so I could pull out my well-worn paperback copy of *Learning French*. I don't know why I wanted to learn French, but I think I felt a need for mental stimulation.

Kent and I committed to seeing that each of our children receive a college education at a private institution. To demonstrate our dedication, Kent gave up cigarettes and, with the savings, we opened a bank account for each child.

Kent's employers were well-recognized companies: Foster-Wheeler, Honeywell, General Electric, Control Data and Magnetic Peripherals. Companies routinely moved rising employees around the country, and we moved seven times over the years. Along the way, we added Nancy and Larry to our family.

One move brought us to sunny Florida, where Kent worked for the space program at Cape Canaveral. There, I became involved with community politics and learned how to motivate people. I became president of the Women's Club, part of the Federated Women's Clubs. Our club was honored nationally during my presidency for a program we initiated for the community library:

Education for Everyone! I presented our story at the national convention. Me! With no college education!

For the first time in my life, I had "free" time on my hands, so I enrolled in a writing course at a local technical college. I don't know why I chose writing, other than the fact I enjoyed reading and loved words. I can't remember what I wrote about, but I recall that the teacher critiqued my paper to the class.

Then Kent was transferred to Oklahoma City. It was a difficult move for all of us. But there was a bigger challenge: I was 40 years old and pregnant!

Well, the world didn't end. We bought a house in the best school district in the city. Kathi and Ed were in high school, Nancy in junior high, and Larry in elementary school. Our little "Okie," Tom, arrived on March 9, 1970.

Now I juggled diapers and formula with college applications for Kathi. Kent and I limited the children to choosing a college within 500 miles of our home, which would be more economical for getting back and forth.

Kathi graduated from high school a year early and went to Grinnell College in Grinnell, Iowa, at 17. She ultimately got a master's degree in library science and a law degree. Our overwhelming sadness was when she was stricken with ovarian cancer and died in 2004. In her will, she left endowments to her schools. There is a climbing wall in Grinnell's gymnasium and a new patio at Washington University Law School that each bear her name. I guess our dedication to education was passed on in our genes, too.

Ed gave the valedictorian address at his high school graduation. I sat in the bleachers listening to Ed speak while keeping Tom, in his little sailor suit, occupied. With Ed, I learned a lot about scholarships and entry requirements for engineering colleges. He received a scholarship to Washington University in St. Louis. After graduation, he moved to California's Silicon Valley, where he works on products for medical markets.

We then had a few years now to think about weddings instead

of colleges, until Nancy's turn came up. I was really getting the hang of scouting out colleges. Texas Christian University in Fort Worth, Texas, seemed a good fit for her and laid the groundwork for her work with patients with eating disorders. Recently, she became an ordained minister.

From an early age, Larry showed artistic ability. An art school was the way to go for him, and we found the Kansas City Art Institute. Today, he owns a model-train business and runs a gallery for other artists. He sometimes lectures at the art institute.

And now we had only our dear Tom at home. By the fifth child, you really are relaxed and know some shortcuts. Finding the best college for him seemed so easy. Tom chose Trinity College in San Antonio. He, too, married his college sweetheart. They lived in Sydney, Australia, before being transferred back to Kansas City.

MY TURN AT LAST

I was in my 50s when my mind once again turned to thoughts of college. This time, for me!

I nervously enrolled in one course at Central State University (now University of Central Oklahoma) in nearby Edmond. Because the only other experience I had besides raising kids was my jobs at the Bethlehem Steel Co., I thought I should take a business course, so I selected marketing. When I entered the first class, I almost ran back to my car. The other students were so young! I felt their stares, but I stayed and completed the course.

The next term, I took two courses. I felt more confident, although the kids still looked at me warily. Nontraditional students were definitely NOT the norm in college classrooms of the late 1970s and early '80s. The following term, I took four courses. I outlined a plan to get a bachelor's degree in liberal arts by the time I was 54. I was drawn to psychology and social studies.

I determined that other students resented my presence in part because I almost always set the curve in my classes and was a "teacher's pet." I was there to learn! Things changed when they found out that I took great shorthand notes and would share them.

FOLLOWING MY INTERESTS

I also used some of my self-taught lessons to further my educational goals. To supplement our income while I was in college, I started a business out of my home. Colors and fabrics had long fascinated me. When I was a teenager, my aunts would pass on their unwanted garments to me. I would be eager to see what treasure they were giving me, but I was frequently disappointed because I somehow knew the colors were not right for me. Even though I didn't have funds for nice clothing when I was growing up, I avidly read fashion magazines at the library. I was—and still am—very fashion conscious. (I really hate admitting that!) At one point, I organized friends who were good seamstresses into a group to create garments for ourselves. I arranged for us to get fabric from a fine store at a discount. We modeled our creations at meetings of the General Electric Wives Club.

A color sense was almost innate with me, but I worked to inform myself further by reading every book I could find on color analysis. I had done a lot of sewing for my daughters and myself, so I had hundreds of fabric remnants, which I sorted into the four color types—Spring, Summer, Autumn, and Winter. I would analyze a client's color type and then create a personal palette of swatches they could take shopping. I named my business Color for You. To advertise, I gave talks to women's groups.

I took a statistics course and wrote a paper on the information I gathered regarding the different color types. My professor was impressed and wanted me to do more work on the paper with the aim of having it published. However, at this point in my life, I just wanted to earn the degrees.

Yes, I said degrees.

I got a bachelor's degree, summa cum laude, when I was 54 years old. To my surprise and joy, our son, Ed and his wife brought their newborn son to my graduation. I don't think there were too many others celebrating their graduation *and* the birth of their first grandchild.

I was bitten by the education bug! I had taken a few undergraduate courses in psychology and wanted to learn more. I entered a master's program, and this time I was in classes with students who more closely resembled my own peer group. I learned quite a bit about myself. I enjoyed administering IQ tests and taping session with pseudo-clients. I completed the master's program, again summa cum laude, when I was 56.

I sat for the state test to become a licensed professional counselor and passed with flying colors. I felt I had something to offer others. I immediately got a job as the parish counselor for a church, then for two parishes. After numerous requests, I opened a private practice in my home. My appointment calendar was full, and it was gratifying to help people make better lives for themselves. I continued counseling individuals and couples until Kent and I retired when I was 62.

We both enjoyed good health, which enabled us to travel and continue learning. We celebrated our 25th anniversary in Budapest, Hungary, where I searched for my roots. Since that first overseas trip, we have traveled to more than 40 countries and have been on every continent except Antarctica. A particularly memorable trip was to the Seychelles, when our daughter Nancy and her husband, Tom, were there with the Peace Corps.

I have sailed down the Yangtze River, taken a gondola ride in Venice, and cruised the Black Sea. I've seen the Eiffel Tower and Big Ben, the majestic opera house in Sydney, and our own national parks. All of this added to my understanding of the universality of humans.

Today, I am an active member of the Osher Lifelong Learning Institute on Furman University campus. This dynamic group is made up primarily of retirees, but there is no age limit for membership. Many instructors are retired professors, but others are hobbyists teaching about their interests. All are unpaid. Kent is teaching a course on nanotechnology. This term there are 90 courses offered through OLLI. Last year, because of the generosity of our members, we dedicated a beautiful new building. We no longer have to travel all over campus; all classes are offered in our own building.

What a privilege it is to be 83, in good health, having celebrated our 60th wedding anniversary, and in an environment that is conducive to even more learning.

Marge Snyder resides in Greenville, South Carolina, where she and Kent retired 20 years ago. During those years, she has enjoyed landscaping and gardening and travel. She also loves playing bridge, reading, and attending Lifelong Learning classes at Furman University. In September 2012, she and Kent celebrated their 60th wedding anniversary with 80 friends and family members. Watching their two granddaughters growing up in Greenville has been a special gift, and the love of their four children and two grandsons an added blessing. She can be reached at snydermarge@aol.com.

ONE IN A MILLION

Reconnecting with a child given up for adoption

Mary Kay Purdy

It was June of 1967 and I felt free. Free of uniforms, free of nuns, free of catechism class. I was elated to graduate from my Catholic high school and was looking forward to starting classes at Ohio State University summer quarter. My sister Karen was already enrolled and managing to get good grades. She was the smart one of the three of us. I was always more interested in making friends and winning their approval.

Almost immediately, I became smitten with a boy who was just about the cutest thing I'd ever seen. I couldn't believe this good-looking college sophomore was interested in me. One thing led to another, and by the time I had my first sexual experience at Christmas, I was in love with this worldly big man on campus.

I began to gain weight but figured I'd just been nibbling too much through my shifts at my bakery job. A girlfriend noticed and said, "You look a little thick around the middle. Do you think you could be pregnant?" I was shocked. But could I be?

As far-fetched as it may seem now, I honestly had no idea that it could possibly be true. I was so naive! I never had "the talk" with my mom. I remember once asking where babies came from and getting an appalled look and a swift change of subject. Girlfriends didn't mention it either, and sex education didn't exist in schools in the 1960s.

A trip to a campus doctor confirmed the unthinkable. I called my boyfriend from a payphone in the lobby and shared my news through tears. He wished me "good luck." I could tell there was no use in begging. I was on my own and in a daze.

An abortion was out of the question; nor did I think I was remotely capable of raising a child alone. Girls weren't raised to believe they could be self-sufficient. Marriage was the goal. In fact, my sister Karen had just married and was already expecting her first child. I knew there would be no support, financial or otherwise, from my working-class family. I was frightened and needed help.

ONLY ONE CHOICE

Being Catholic and unwed, there was only one possible avenue: I would surrender my child for adoption. A friend suggested I visit Catholic Social Services as a place to start. I went to their offices alone and met with a woman I will never forget. She was friendly and hopeful and the most beautiful woman I'd ever seen. More important, she did not judge me. She calmly offered information about St. Joseph Infant and Maternity Home near Cincinnati. I was so grateful.

The next step would be to tell my parents. My mother was deeply religious and I remember her sobs of disappointment. But after a few strong admonishments, she hugged me and said, "We'll get through this."

Telling my father was more difficult. Dad had a heart condition and was prone to sudden violent outbursts. As I began my story, he walked around the table with a grimace on his face and collapsed at my feet. I thought I had killed him! Fortunately, I had not, but the episode added tremendously to my guilt. I knew I would be damned to hell for sure. At the same time, I couldn't help but notice the striking contrast: Just a few months earlier, my family had been celebrating the news of Karen's pregnancy. But my pregnancy brought only pain and sadness.

A few days later my mother drove me to Cincinnati and dropped me off for an extended stay at the "home."

Because the 1960s were a time when appearances were more important than anything, I was to wait out the eventual birth and adoption of my baby in a strange place rather than face the disgrace of raising a child that was not the result of wedded bliss. Families, and mine was no exception, felt so ashamed when their "good girl" became a pregnant "bad girl." It didn't matter that I was still a child myself and had never been away from home before.

My life at St. Joe's is a blur. I remember that the nuns in charge were the Sisters of Charity. It housed about 15 pregnant girls and approximately 30 babies considered "unadoptable" because of various medical conditions. It was our job to spend four hours a day caring for these babies. It was a blessing to cuddle and love those little angels.

We went by first names only. A few girls, like me, were there for several months. It was a revolving door as girls arrived, delivered and left. If you were close friends with a girl who was ready to deliver, you got to go along on a wild ride—a very big deal, considering we otherwise never got to go out. A trip to Good Samaritan Hospital was a harrowing experience. The nuns would drive at break-neck speed to get there on time, with veils trailing out the window of the station wagon. On one trip I witnessed a newborn being handed to her mother who was just wheeled out of delivery. The father was at her side. The doctor said, "She is perfect, 10 fingers and 10 toes." My heart sank to my stomach and I cried because I could not imagine a happier ending.

My mom and sister came for a surprise visit in August. They brought Karen's new baby, Barbara. I held her close, in total awe, as I said to my pregnant girlfriends, "Look, it's a real baby!" meaning that she was a "keeper."

In September, when it was my time for the fateful trip to the hospital, I remember being so frightened. The only information we received about the birthing process was from the nuns. They were lovely women, but not exactly forthcoming about what we could expect. However, they insisted it was best not to see the child after delivery.

I woke up in a ward of six women with a nurse standing by my bed. She said very sweetly, "You have a beautiful little girl with blond hair and blue eyes." I sobbed knowing this was the only information I would ever have about her. I called my mother and said, "It's over, Mom." But in reality, it was just the beginning.

A week later my dad came to pick me up. He was such a gentleman. He carried my bags and opened my car door. I hadn't been outside of the home in four months, except to go to the hospital, and I hadn't seen my father since the day I almost killed him. We went to lunch at a restaurant called the Windjammer and both tried so hard to make polite conversation. My sister told me that she once heard Dad say, "I've never felt so sorry for anyone in my life."

Back home, no one asked how I felt or where I'd been. A few did send anonymous letters addressed to "Virgin Mary Kay," which were devastating to receive. Counseling wasn't offered or probably even thought of. I was supposed to just get over it and move on. Don't think about it. Pretend it didn't happen. My family even watched me closely with Karen's baby and took Barbara from me if it seemed I was holding her too close for too long. It was a recipe sure to make a young girl feel unworthy and to believe that what she did was very wrong. But I couldn't quit thinking about that "beautiful little girl with blond hair and blue eyes."

JOURNEY OF RECOVERY

After 15 years of a rather reckless life of experimentation intermixed with attempts at normalcy, I had an epiphany. I realized that I was not just a "bad girl" going to hell for an unforgivable sin. I was successful in my jobs and I had friends who loved and supported me. I began to see that I had value. I embarked on a journey of recovery.

I started by coming out. I began telling people in similar situations about the baby I gave up for adoption. It was freeing to rid myself of the shame associated with the secrecy. Although regaining my self-esteem and self-approval took years, I would discover that this was the easy part. Knowing I had a daughter somewhere who I never held or even laid eyes on continued to haunt me. I eventually married and had hopes of a "replacement baby," but my husband didn't want children. I resigned myself to a childless life.

I had a burning need to know about my daughter and that I'd made the right decision in surrendering her. I began the process to find her when she would have been 19 years old; however, I decided that it would be too disruptive for her at that point in her life. Did she even know she was adopted? I backed off. But when she turned 30 I felt the time was right. I met with an organization called Reunite, and they were quickly able to put the pieces together. Adoption records are sealed, but after only a few meetings a woman slipped a piece of paper into my hand with three names. One of them was my daughter's. When I discovered which name was hers and where she lived, I decided that the least intimidating approach would be to write a letter.

Dear Rosanne,

My name is Mary Kay Purdy. I respectfully and humbly ask you to read the following letter and I ask you to keep an open mind and heart while doing so. Please know that it is sent to you in love and with great concern that I may be overwhelming you with the information contained herein.

On September 25, 1968, I gave birth to a baby girl. After many phone calls, Internet searches, letters and conversations with organizations dedicated to reuniting people, I have been told that you are the woman I gave birth to almost 31 years ago.

I will never be able to explain to you my feelings just knowing that you are alive and well. All these years I have prayed for your well-being and happiness. I have particularly thought about you as each of your birthdays passed. Many times since your birth I have lamented and cried for the loss of you, knowing how you would have enriched my life.

I am hoping with all my heart that you are open to hearing this information. I am hoping with all my heart that I have not told you something that you never expected to hear, but that it is something you were waiting to hear. I am hoping that you believe me when I tell you that my only intention is to get to know you and to answer any questions you may have about me, my family, or the circumstances surrounding my decision so many years ago.

It is with great anticipation and love that I await hearing from you.

A few weeks later, Rosanne called. Her voice was music to my ears. I now understood what "walking on air" meant. She had known she was adopted for as long as she could remember. She had wonderful loving parents. Her brother was also adopted. She was married and had three children.

COMING FULL CIRCLE

Because Rosanne was a devoted mother she understood my need to connect with her. More than that, she was kind, open, loving, and nonjudgmental. In six months she was ready to meet me. We met at a small restaurant near her home. I cannot find words to describe my reaction to looking into her eyes for the first time. I saw my own face looking back. We were the same height, with the same smile and even the same dimples.

I didn't know if she'd ever want to see me again, so I took her a gift in a velvet-lined box. Inside was a gold pendant necklace that had belonged to her great-grandmother, a beaded handbag from the 1930s that had belonged to my mother, and a beautiful glass paperweight that was mine. I wanted her to know that she had always been loved from afar and had a rich heritage of strong, wonderful German women.

I always said that if Rosanne had stated that she didn't have room for me in her life I would have respected her request. It would have been enough to know that she was happy and well cared for. But being able to live my life without secrets or shame and to participate in her life is more than I ever allowed myself to imagine.

Rosanne did accept me into her life, and for the last 13 years, I have had a wonderful relationship with my daughter and her children. She and I talk on the phone almost daily and she and the kids visit for a week in the summer and at Christmas. I don't try to be Rosanne's mother. She has one whom she loves deeply. But I know I have a special place as her birth mother and I cherish our relationship. We sometimes deal with awkward moments when roles and boundaries are ambiguous, but we love each other and our lives have been greatly enriched by knowing one another.

I have also thanked her parents for doing what I could not: raise and care for my daughter. I met them at their granddaughter's first communion a couple of years after we connected. I knew her father was disappointed with my appearance in Rosanne's life, so I slipped a note into her mother's purse in an attempt to explain.

Dear Mr. and Mrs. H.,

I am humbled and grateful to finally meet you both. It is an honor for me to look into the eyes of the wonderful people who loved, reared and raised the child I gave up for adoption many years ago. I thank you from the very bottom of my heart for your love and devotion to that child.

I sincerely hope you understand that my need to know about Rosanne centered on my confirming that I made the right decision, when at age 18, I gave her up for adoption. For 30 years I wondered if she had loving parents who were able to provide for her. She is truly a wonderful woman and devoted mother and a tribute to your love and attention as her parents. You are everything I had wished for her and more.

The fact that I am able to have a relationship with Rosanne and her beautiful children at this stage of my life is beyond my wildest dreams.

Meeting you now closes the circle on that period of my life. Thank you again for sharing your beautiful daughter with me.

Rosanne's mother was unbelievably kind and responded to my note with one I will cherish forever.

Dear Mary Kay~

What a joy it was to meet you! Our meeting was just as I knew it would be because I have come to know you through Rosanne. It was a very special time we shared with you, warm and rewarding for us.

I used to tell Rosanne the story of her adoption every year on the anniversary of the day we brought her home. I always said that her birth mother was a very good person "because look how good you are!" I would continue, "Your birth mother did the most generous, most loving, most giving and the very hardest thing that she'll ever do in surrendering you for adoption. She did that because she knew that she could not give you what she knew you would need. She did that for your good, for your benefit, for your future because she loved you. She gave the greatest gift to you; she gave you life.

I have to say that I am so happy to know you, Mary Kay, through Rosanne up till now, and now in person.

Be at peace, Mary Kay. We are.

With love from one mother to another.

Now I ask you, what more could I possibly ask for? How wonderful that what was once so painful was now so joyful.

A few years ago, at my daughter's urging, I began a search for her birth father. I eventually found him through Facebook. I asked if he remembered me and told him that a special person would like to meet him. To my surprise, he agreed to meet us at a restaurant on the interstate.

He said he didn't remember my phone call from the doctor's office and that he'd never tried to contact me. "What happened was just the way it was back then," he said. His wife knew that he'd fathered a child but his three children did not. He asked Rosanne if she had any questions and we spent an hour in casual conversation. Rosanne has since tried to contact him, but he ignores her requests. I don't hold a grudge against him. It was a long time ago and he was a kid, too. However, it's amazing to think that this event that shaped my entire life had no consequence for him, then or now.

I am without a doubt a lucky woman, blessed beyond measure. I have only one regret: I'm sorry that my wonderful mother, Lucille Daub Purdy, never met the child she loved and prayed for daily.

TAKING THE LEAP!

Recently I attended the screening of the documentary *A Girl Like Her* by Ann Fessler. It's about the one million girls forced to surrender their children for adoption in the 1950s and '60s. I attended with a woman I had not seen in 44 years, not since we were at St. Joseph Infant and Maternity Home together. Kim had been "found" by her son two years earlier. She kept her secret for 42 years.

I sincerely hope that some of the one million women who had similar experiences and who are still holding onto the secrecy and shame consider opening that door. I believe that living with truth ultimately hurts no one. Their lives can be improved immeasurably by simply sharing their stories and if telling my story helps just one woman make that leap, it would be a wonderful outcome.

Mary Kay Purdy recently graduated from the Institute of Holistic Health Careers in Columbus, Ohio, as a Registered Polarity Therapy Practitioner and Corporate Wellness Coach. She retired from Ohio state government in 2010 after having served in many capacities, including as an information technology project manager for Job and Family Services and manager of Constituent Affairs in the governor's office. She enjoys living a healthy and happy lifestyle in her family homestead in German Village among her friends, family, and her dog Mr. Maxx. Her daughter, Rosanne, and her grandchildren live near Cleveland, Ohio, and remain the light of Mary Kay's life.

ADOPTION:
A RELATIVE COMEDY

*Re-defining my existence after meeting
my biological mother*

Sarah Elizabeth Greer

While most newborns go home with the person who gave birth to them, I left the hospital with an Amish family. And during that time, my name was Amy Yost. Luckily, that arrangement lasted for only three months. Then I was transferred to the Greers, where I became a bona fide *Greer Whisperer*.

I was like a dog whisperer or horse whisperer—those able to understand and communicate in an otherworldly way with another species. For me, it was with genetically disparate humans who were wired completely different from me. But I prided myself on being able to detect and decipher all the psychological and emotional nuances of my family of Greer: John, Connie and Jonathan, the three greatest loves of my life, forever and ever, 'til death do us part.

HYPER-VIGILANCE:
1. An enhanced state of sensory sensitivity accompa-nied by an exaggerated intensity of behaviors whose purpose is to detect threats.

The only two words you need to remember from that definition are exaggerated intensity. That's me in a nutshell. And it describes the high stakes way I dealt with my Greers.

I remember the time in seventh grade when my friend Michelle Lewis invited me to dinner. When I called home to ask permission, my father replied with something that sounded very alarming: "Let me go ask your mother. *She's taking a nap.*" OH MY GOD! SHE'S TAKING A NAP! My stomach felt like it would explode and my chest hurt. Why was my mother taking a nap? She must be sick. I panicked.

"Dad! What's wrong?"

"Nothing. She's tired."

"I don't believe you!" I screamed. "If everything is okay, hold the phone to her mouth and tell her to say 'Everything's okay'!"

He took the phone to where she was snoozing peacefully on the sofa. "Connie, is everything okay?"

"Johhhhn, why did you wake me?"

"Sarah's worried about you."

I heard her sigh. "I'm taking a cat nap!"

I was on the floor of the Lewis' kitchen at this point, nursing a nosebleed and reeling with nausea. Mrs. Lewis was on the floor with me, holding tightly to my hand. From the way I was acting, she thought my mother must have had a heart attack or been in a terrible accident.

I shouted, "Dad, if everything is *truly* okay with mom, tell her to say, 'Everything's okay'!"

Poor dad. He relayed my message. "Sarah wants you to say 'Everything's okay, Connie' if you are just taking a nap out of exhaustion instead of something more serious."

My mother knew the code.

"EVERYTHING'S OKAY!" she shouted.

And just like that, my stomach stopped hurting and I could enjoy dinner with the Lewis family.

Most adoptees possess this quality of hyper-vigilance, but it is a trait most often linked to post traumatic stress disorder.

IMPACTS OF ADOPTION

Babies given up for adoption perceive the loss of their biological mothers almost immediately. People say, "No way! How can that be?" But consider this: The baby has spent nine months inside the woman's body, hearing her voice and connecting to her every emotion and hormonal change—laughter, sorrow, stress. The two are connected by an umbilical cord. Of course the baby recognizes the woman is missing! Textbooks call this phenomenon in adopted children a "primal wound." Supposedly, it's a hole in their hearts, a pervasive feeling of not being enough, because they haven't had the opportunity to be loved by their biological mother.

It is said that when a baby experiences the disconnection from seeing, hearing, smelling and tasting all evidence of where she comes from, she experiences a shock called *susto* or *soul fright,* a loss so great the soul is shocked out of the body. This is what happened to me. In essence, on the day I was born, I experienced the loss of everything I knew to be true. I lost all connection to my biological roots, to my history, the reasoning behind my impulses and personality traits and, most of all, to my original mother.

We learn how to be human through relationships, and my first relationship disappeared. This created trauma to my brain. And the brain is an historical organ. It stores all of our life experiences, even from the womb. In essence, when I was born with nobody to receive and recognize me, I experienced stress at the level of trauma. I was left with an incomplete narrative of who I was. This filled me with a sorrow I have carried throughout my life, a "disenfranchised grief" that isn't recognized by society as something to grieve about.

But there's a miracle in all of this, illustrated by these two sayings:

1. There is nothing so whole as a broken heart.
2. The crack, the wound, is where the light shines through.

In exchange for *susto*, I was given the gift of empathy. I psychically feel other people's pain and loneliness. The person whose pain I feel most is my mother's. Connie Greer is everybody's caretaker, with nobody to care for *her*. She had to overcome huge disappointments and tiny tragedies to escape her past and have a family of her own. And I think it is absolutely no accident that I became her daughter. To me, it's ironic that she always told me that I was chosen. I know it was the other way around: I chose my mother. Her destiny and mine were meant to collide. And our journey to be together made it all the more extraordinary.

I spent my youth trying to create "perfect" mother/daughter moments. I pretended that we were being videotaped in front of a live studio audience, and I tried to create magical scenarios to show how lucky we were to have each other. For example, if I noticed that my father made her cry, which he often did, I would think, "The studio audience needs to see how beautifully I can curl my mother's hair." And then I would curl her hair until the panic left my chest, until she smiled again.

I like to think that Connie Greer and I were a mother-and-daughter team of solo artists, thrown together to help each other make sense of our destiny; human beings in a soul contract, struggling to find happiness, etching out a reason for being on this earth. My mother accomplished this by being a complete realist. I was the exact opposite: I love fantasy. Unreality and disillusionment were my two middle names.

My mother was practical and no-nonsense, and most days she couldn't tolerate my antics. We were also *energetically* opposites. She was always saying, "Sarah, stop talking so loudly. And, for god's sake, cool your jets, kid. You're like a bull in a china shop!"

I knew she loved me, but she didn't understand me. She couldn't. So, in an effort to appease her, I became a servile, self-abnegating and ingratiating perfectionist. I won awards and starred in my high-school plays. I went to bible school and memorized verses. I joined 4-H and learned how to cross-stitch.

But a leopard can't change its spots. On the day I was fired from my job as a wench at the Pennsylvania Renaissance Faire for diving head first, in full costume, into the mud pit, my mother was apoplectic. "Sarah!" she yelled, "You wonder why people think of you as 'el weirdo,' and I'm telling you it's because you have no credibility! People don't take you seriously because you don't take yourself seriously!"

That sent me to the dictionary:

CREDIBLE:
1. Capable of being believed; believable.
2. Worthy of belief or confidence; trustworthy.

It hit me hard, but she had a point. I had always felt very low self worth. How could I be worthy of belief? I was invisible. I wasn't real. For as long as I could remember, I had been a misunderstood human being, raised to resist my natural instincts on a daily basis.

Being adopted filled me with shame. I hated the word *adopted* and still do. It filled me with a shame I couldn't articulate and sliced my heart like a knife knowing that I had come from another mommy's tummy and had then been given away. I was sure this was because she didn't have the money to keep me. I felt sorry for her, whoever she was. She did the right thing, though, because I had the best family in the world. I wished her well. But I didn't miss her. And I definitely didn't want to know her.

I never wanted to meet my Bio. Ever. Ewwwww. What kind of woman could carry a baby in her womb and then give her away to biological aliens? A poor soul, that's what. Every night I got down on my knees and thanked God for the Greers. They were my precious angels, and I knew that nothing could ever change the close-knit, safe and solid alliance we had.

Then she found me.

I had read those four words before, while I was reading an Elinor Lipman novel on this very subject. But it was a work of FICTION, and I remember thinking to myself, "That never happens."

Even though it's been 21 years, I am only now getting a grip on the impact being found by my biological mother has had on my life. I want toss back my head and bellow an anguished scream, a laugh mixed with a cry of such grief, complexity and raw passion that it would frighten you. Then I'd throw myself to the ground and pour bucket after bucket of water over my head, like Electra did in Aeschylus's *The Libation Bearers*.

Turns out I'm Greek.

And it was Aeschylus who said: "He who learns must suffer, and, even in our sleep, pain that cannot forget falls drop by drop upon the heart, and in our own despair, against our will, comes wisdom to us by the awful grace of God."

Hello, Awakening!
Welcome, Epiphany!
Let the lessons begin.

ON BEING FOUND BY MY BIO

The first time I heard my biological mother's voice was on the telephone at 8 p.m. on January 12, 1991. The only way to translate the effects of that call is to compare it to a deaf person suddenly able to hear or a blind person who suddenly sees. It exhilarated me. It changed what I knew to be real. It upended my sanity. It devastated me. I didn't expect to recognize her voice, but I did. I was wired to remember her voice, her zany humor, her over-the-top wild-woman essence.

My biological mother's name is Susan Mastros Dohner. She fell in love with my biological father at the age of 12. One night when they were 15 and 16, they got hot and heavy while watching the horror movie *The Man with a Thousand Faces* starring Lon Chaney, and I was conceived. It was the first time they ever had sex. She didn't tell anyone she was pregnant until one week before I was born.

The first time I met my maker was on March 30, 1991, the day before Easter, the day symbolizing Jesus Christ's resurrection from the dead. And now it also symbolized mine. Because on the day that I first looked into her eyes, a death took place. It was the death of the me I had adapted myself to be and of everything that came before. Then I rose from the dead and was reborn. I became real.

Sue is a totally outrageous woman, and we are kindred spirits. We both fell to the floor in the same way when we laughed. We shared the same mannerisms, the same over-the-top absurdity, the same sense of making magical moments out of the ordinary. Instead of telling each other stories about our families, we would create re-enactments of our most important life moments, acting them out over and over and over as we laughed and laughed and laughed. I've never done drugs, but being with her felt like being on drugs. And I couldn't get enough. My soul was being called back into my body. My soul was coming back to her.

There was one thing about my biological mother that set her apart from anyone I had ever met in my life: she was hysterically funny, a bang-your-hands-on-the-table hilarious clown.

Being funny was her defense mechanism to hide her pain. She didn't want her family to suffer, so she'd perform a pratfall or mime an invisible baton-twirling routine. But I could see right through her; I could feel her pain. She was overcompensating for her shame and her "ambiguous loss"—the unfinished business of surrendering me, a loss that could not be openly mourned or socially supported. And here's the thing: I could not have recognized this ambiguity in her if I hadn't first recognized my own. We were merging in our trauma, participating in a mirror exercise of the soul.

What happened next was that I fell down a rabbit hole; I became lost as a character in my own life story. I could see only the tragedy.

Meeting my biological mother interrupted the natural order of things. I realized that everything I once defined as true or real with my Greers had not merely vanished, but had been only a construct for survival in the first place. Being found by Sue ripped all aspects of my identity to shreds. I saw myself as a fraud. I no longer knew who I was.

And how was I going to assimilate my Greers into my new reality of epic biological understanding and kinship? Why did I suddenly feel so disconnected from them?

My parents wanted to give me space. They were suffering but didn't want me to know. My mother was devastated, but she acted like my being found by my bio was like winning the lottery. She, like me and Sue, had now landed her safe little bubble on The Planet of Disenfranchised, Ambiguous Grief. And don't think any aspect of her unresolved sorrow, resulting from *her* loss of *her* daughter, had been lost on me.

For several years, I was in shock. It was the beginning of my Hero's Journey, but instead of looking for a way to accept what was now true and move forward, I resisted. I made it my mission to chase answers to deeply existential questions. I went on a 20-year spiritual quest. I traveled, researched, wrote, explored, performed and mourned.

I became enamored of the work of the French writer/visual and conceptual artist Sophie Calle, who created narratives using images and texts from her interactions with strangers. I thought it was like what I had been doing for 20 years with both of my families—collecting objects, slides, videos, answering-machine messages and letters—to make sense of who I was. And now I was ready to turn it into a narrative and share it. But how?

I studied the art of comedy, and learned that high stakes equals funny, so I was right at home. One night I was in a class at Stand-Up NY for women comediennes. The teacher, a recovering alcoholic, ran his classes like an AA meeting. "Ladies," he said, "you are only as sick as your secrets." He then instructed us to reveal a deep, dark secret about ourselves. Every woman who got onstage revealed a horrifying fact about herself—date rape, incestuous relationship…the list of hellish secrets was moving and powerful. But because of the high stakes involved, each story was naturally funny.

When it was my turn, I blurted out, "I'm adopted!" I started weeping uncontrollably and fell to my knees like only an over-the-top Greek drama queen can, and out of my mouth came all sorts of crazy confessions. The other women were screaming with laughter. My teacher, tears running down his face, was pounding the table. The more they laughed, the more I shared. I got a standing ovation and learned the power of sharing a tragic story in a funny way. It has the power to heal both the teller and the listener and transform both in the process.

I knew what my game in life was going to be: To use this power of storytelling to show people that I could rescue my life and re-tell it in a way that changed my destiny—and so could they. I created a one-woman show: part stand-up comedy and part storytelling, an art installation mixed with image and text, a la Sophie Calle.

Between 1999 and 2001, I crafted and performed *BIO-HAZARD* as part of a solo performance workshop at the Westbeth Theatre Center in New York City. In November 2001, I performed the work as part of Ensemble Studio Theatre's Oktoberfest, with Karen Trott directing. I mounted it as a 90-minute work-in-progress during the HA! Comedy Festival. The stories continued to be told in a variety of small downtown New York venues over the next few years, which led to two staged readings (directed by Valentina Fratti) in September 2005 as part of the Artists of Tomorrow Series produced by Six Figures Theatre Co. in New York City. In 2009 I performed a Virginia Scott-directed version of *BIO-HAZARD* at The Peoples Improv Theater to sold-out crowds. The show climaxed with a surprise appearance by my biological mother, who joined me onstage for a baton-twirling routine and to teach the audience a Greek dance.

Having Sue appear was life-altering and brought about a new vision for the show: to call it *BIO-HAZARD: (a relative comedy)* and invite *both* of my mothers to join me onstage. I wanted to create a piece of theater in which all three of us take a stand for each other, showing that love is stronger than fear and shame. It's a one-of-a-kind reality show, allowing the audience to experience both nature and nurture up close and personal.

I created a Kickstarter campaign that raised $18,000. Then I wrote a new incarnation of the script and entered it into the International United Solo Festival, the largest solo festival in the world. It was accepted and slated to debut on Nov. 13, 2012.

I had never performed my story in front of my adoptive mother and was terrified to share my truth with her. But both Sue and Connie came to New York and sat on my bed as I stammered through my script. They loved it! And then a crazy thing happened: my fear vanished. I let go of all of the hesitation and apology that had been living inside my heart and connected with my audience.

Five days later, my play won best comedy of the festival!

The show has symbolized my awakening to my spiritual connection to the universe. I have found a way to rescue the story of my life from one of tragedy and re-tell it as a divine comedy. The act of doing this with my mothers shifted my reality and called my soul back to my body. It is my soul's calling. Literally.

If our words really do create our world, consider this possibility: It was my fate to be given up for adoption, but my destiny is up to me. I have embraced myself fully and now live by the motto "Be who you were meant to be." I make up my own definitions these days.

ECCENTRIC:
1. One that deviates markedly from an established norm, especially a person of odd or unconventional behavior.
2. To be whimsical, outlandish, a bit daft, wacko. Have a moonflaw in the brain, have a screw loose.

Those were taken from the dictionary, but this next one's all mine:

ECCENTRIC:
A person who follows her higher path.

Sarah Elizabeth Greer is an actress, playwright, memoirist, and solo performer whose game in life is magical connection, empowerment, and touching humanity through humor, silly fun, and deep sharing. Sarah is a graduate of The William Esper Studio and holds a B.A. in Theater from Mount Holyoke College. She is a proud member of The Dramatist's Guild, PEN American Center, and the American Adoption Congress. She is currently working on a two-volume memoir inspired by The Eleusinian Mysteries and is in the process of creating a TV series based on her solo show. She can be reached at segreer80@aol.com

A NEW KIND OF NORMAL

A daughter fights for her family when their world is turned upside down

Kim Davis

Life is short, and your world can be turned upside-down in a moment. Those may be clichés, but I know their messages to be true. These are the difficult lessons I learned when I was only 14 years old.

I was blessed to have two parents who exemplified what a strong, caring relationship should be. They had many friends, and our home was often filled with music and laughter. When our folks were entertaining, my brother, Murell, and I would sneak out of bed and sit at the top of the stairs to eavesdrop and watch the grownups dance. Eventually we'd be discovered, and Dad would ask me to dance. I loved this when I was a kid, but heading into my teen years, it became a little embarrassing. He would ask anyway and, yes, I would accept.

Quiet times were special too. Mom and Dad enjoyed each other's company and talked about everything from current events to their dreams for the future. They didn't hide their respect or devotion for one another, and our whole family was affectionate. As kids, Murell and I would eagerly wait for Dad's arrival each afternoon. When the door opened, we'd jump into his arms and shower him with hugs and kisses.

Dad was an engineer. He could fix anything, and he loved to build things, like the bicycle he made out of old parts from the junkyard. Mom had been educated as a nurse, but she worked for an airline. Despite both being employed, they always made sure one of them was home to look after Murell and me; Dad worked days and Mom evenings. And we always sat down for family dinner, with each of us sharing something about our day.

But one spring day, everything changed.

FINDING MYSELF ALONE

Murell and I were in school, and my mom tells me that she and Dad, who was off work that day, were discussing upcoming plans. I didn't know it at the time, but Dad had accepted a new job, and we would soon be leaving our home in Detroit for San Francisco. While they were talking, my mother noticed that my father's speech was slurring, and the left side of his face drooped. From her medical training, she realized Dad was having a stroke. She immediately called 911, and he was rushed to the hospital.

I was a freshman in high school, and I rode public transportation to and from school. The bus dropped me off about a block from my house, and as I got closer, I noticed cars in our driveway. I knew at once that something was wrong. As soon as I entered the front door, my mom told me the terrible news: Dad had had a stroke and a heart attack. Fortunately, she said, the prognosis was good. Because he was young—47 years old—and had no history of health problems, the doctors expected him to recover.

Dad was improving, so my mother was looking into a rehab specialist for the minor paralysis he had suffered. Then my father's brain began to swell and he lapsed into a coma.

My mother requested that my brother and I be allowed to visit Dad in the hospital. I received permission, but despite Mom's begging, Murell, who was only 7, did not. He has never gotten over this. Seeing my dad, who was always so vibrant and full of life, in that condition was surreal. All I could do was hold his hand and tell him I loved him. After seven days in the hospital, my dad passed away on June 17, two days after my 14th birthday.

Because my mother wanted to keep our lives as normal as possible, we continued to go to school during Dad's hospitalization. So once again, as I was walking home from the bus stop, I saw all the cars. My maternal grandfather, who had come to stay with us, gave me the news. I remember feeling numb; again, the situation just did not seem real.

At that time of my life, I had never heard of any kids who had lost a parent. I didn't even have friends who had lost a grandparent. The days following my Dad's death were a whirlwind. It was decided that the funeral would be in my parents' home state of Kentucky.

My brother and I had always spent a few weeks in the summer visiting our maternal grandparents, but we didn't know our father's parents as well. Dad was a child of divorce, and his parents did not get along. Plus, they never seemed very comfortable around us. Even at the funeral they were distant, although I could see that they were both devastated by the loss of their only child.

When we returned home, it was the beginning of summer vacation. I went to visit some of my neighborhood friends. They extended their sympathies, but then we just kind of stared at each other. As an adult, I realize that they were grieving my dad too, and they were unsure what to do because they had never been in a similar situation. It was probably scary for them to know that something like that could happen to their own parents. But I recall that it was a lonely summer for me.

Back at school in the fall, everyone handled me like I was going to break. I'd notice a lot of whispering and pointing when I'd walk down the halls, and the teachers seemed overly protective. All I wanted was to be treated the same way I was before my dad died, but it took a while before things returned to normal.

My mother put Murell and me in a group counseling program for children who lost a parent. Each week, we'd sit in a circle and, one by one, share how we were feeling. I really hated the sessions, mostly because I wasn't really sure how I felt. Sometimes I didn't feel anything, but I had to come up with something so the counselor would stop probing. I finally told my mother I didn't want to go anymore, and she didn't pressure me to return. Although I was still devastated, I grieved on my own.

My mother, too, was also dealing with a lot, suddenly raising two young children alone. She took a six-month leave of absence from her job so she could focus on putting our lives back together. I would often hear her crying in her bedroom late at night, but other than at the funeral, she never cried in front of us. I think she felt that if she maintained a strong front, it would be easier for us to cope. Instead, it reinforced the belief that it was not okay to show our feelings.

Over the next few months, Mom began to change. She never wanted to leave the house, and she became suspicious of everything and everyone. I once invited over a girl who had never been to our home before. She and I were in a couple of classes together and had begun to develop a close relationship. When I discovered that she lived nearby, I asked her to come by after school to hang out. My mother took one look at her and told her that she had to leave immediately and not come back. Mom said my friend was "not to be trusted." Even though we would say hello in class, the girl and I never spoke of the incident. What could I say? Even I didn't understand why my mom acted the way she did. I was humiliated and stopped inviting any friends over.

Then Mom began not trusting certain foods. Some days, she would cook dinner for Murell and me, and then determine that the food had been poisoned and not allow us to eat it. I knew something was happening to my mother, but I didn't know what it was or what to do about it. My brother was only 7, so I couldn't talk to him about it. Even now, he doesn't remember much about that time in our lives.

Mom's friends would stop by the house to check on her, and I would try to explain to them that my mom had changed. But because she was still "functioning"—paying bills, getting my brother and me to school in the morning—they would tell me not to worry. Mom was just missing my dad, they'd say, and she would be all right.

SEEKING HELP

Finally, I called my mom's father. He came right away. Only a day after he arrived, he knew my mom wasn't well. Because his wife had died eight years earlier, he understood the pain of losing a spouse. He talked to Mom and got her to open up about her feelings. He stayed with us for two months, and it brought me great comfort. There was finally an adult in the house who could "fix" whatever was wrong. And slowly Mom began to come around. It was a huge relief to see life returning to normal.

The peace didn't last long. Seven months after my dad died, we got a call about his mother. She was in the final stages of pancreatic cancer. Due to the strained relationship between my mother and grandmother, no one had contacted us sooner. We flew to Kentucky to be with my grandmother, but by then she had been intubated and unable to speak. All she could do was squeeze my mom's hand. My mother asked her if there was something she wanted to say, and my grandmother would nod her head. Sadly, we never found out what it was, and she passed away soon after. Another death, another funeral.

My mother was doing her best to move on. She returned to work and was reconnecting with friends. I was starting to relax when something else happened. We got a call that my dad's father had died of a heart attack, six months after my grandmother. In a span of 14 months, I had lost my entire family on my father's side. My mother was in no condition to go to another funeral, so we simply went to the funeral home without anyone's knowledge and quietly paid our respects.

One friend, unhappy that Mom wasn't her old self yet, told her that she thought Mom was "stronger than this" and she should have "bounced back." Mom took it hard, and shortly after being chastised, she started changing again.

One morning she said she wasn't feeling well and stayed home from work. When I got home from school, she had regressed to acting like a child. She was sitting in the family room, still in her nightgown and calling me "Mom." I tried to explain to her that she was my mother, but she kept insisting that she was a little girl. I told her that she needed to get bathed and dressed, and she responded that she didn't know how. I helped her upstairs, ran her bath water, washed her, and put her in bed.

Then I called my grandfather, but due to health issues, he couldn't come right away. One of my mother's siblings told me that my mother was just acting this way to get attention. I knew that wasn't true and stopped talking to anyone except my grandfather.

Days went by and my mother's behavior became totally erratic. She wasn't sleeping and would pace the floor all hours of the night. She was paranoid. Her speech became rapid and frenzied, and she would rant about things that had never happened. For example, she told people that she worked for the FBI and was investigating a case.

I was completely responsible for looking out for my brother.

I would get him up and ready for school in the mornings and made sure he ate dinner in the evenings. As my mother's mental health deteriorated, I was afraid to leave her home alone. What could I do? I had to go to school. But my instincts had been right. I came home one day and learned that she had been standing on the front porch screaming at the top of her lungs. Fortunately, a caring neighbor took her inside, but that is when I knew I had to do something.

I again called my grandfather, and he came that weekend with my aunt and two uncles. By the time her family arrived, Mom was irrational. My grandfather told her that she needed to go to the hospital for treatment, but she refused, saying nothing was wrong with her. We had to trick her by saying we wanted to take her for a ride. As we drove, Mom talked non-stop, not making any sense. I was both scared and anxious, and my eyes filled with tears. As we approached the emergency room entrance and my mother realized where we were, she began kicking and screaming and fighting to get away. It took both of my uncles to restrain her until a hospital attendant could come and assist. People in the emergency room were staring at us as we walked in, and I was both embarrassed and angry—not just at the people gaping at us, but also at my mother for being the way she was.

Mom was taken to the psychiatric ward. By that time, she had become psychotic, and no longer recognized anyone. She was yelling and screaming. They gave her an antipsychotic drug to calm her down and placed her in a padded room so she couldn't harm herself or others. The doctor told us that if Mom did not respond to the medication within 24 hours she may never be well again because she had remained untreated for so long. My grandfather held me tight and told me that everything was going to be all right. I think that was the longest 24 hours of my life. I cried and prayed.

When I returned to the hospital the next afternoon, I was

grateful to see that, although she was still not herself, my mother was no longer psychotic. She remained in the hospital for seven days, and before she left, the doctor provided a diagnosis: bipolar disorder brought on by extreme stress.

I had no clue what bipolar disorder was, but I knew it was serious. I also recognized that this information was not something I could openly share with others. During this time, there was no one I could talk to about what was going on in my life. How many other 15-year-olds had lost so many family members in such a short time? Or had a parent suffering from mental illness? I was embarrassed about my life and afraid of what might happen next. I worried about whether my family would survive.

My mother had taught me an important lesson: Any time you don't know something, look it up. That's what I started to do. I researched how to handle grief and learned more about mental illness. For a while, the more I learned, the more afraid I became. My stability had been shaken, and I lived in fear that my mother might die. I also was afraid that I might develop mental illness. Why did this happen? Hadn't we been through enough? It was all too much.

My mother was seeing a psychiatrist and, on medication, she began to get better.

STARTING ANEW, CARRYING THE OLD

But it was a long road to recovery. She sold our home in Michigan, and we lived with her father in Kentucky for six months before she was well enough to buy a new house. It took my mother another year before she seemed normal to me. But eventually, she returned to work, and I went to college.

Even as my life was improving, I was left with the shame of what had happened. I carried that with me into my early 30s. During those years, I didn't tell friends about my mother's illness, except occasionally in a very summarized version. Because of the stigma that surrounds mental illness, I was—and sometimes still am—hesitant to share my past. Not until six months before my wedding, at my mother's insistence, did I even tell my fiancé the details of my past. I was relieved to learn that it didn't change his feelings about me or my family.

It still pains me to see how people with mental illness, who are fully treatable and can lead normal lives, are thought of as inferior by our society. They live in fear of being "found out." My mother worked until retirement without further incident, but she was always afraid that her diagnosis of so many years earlier would be discovered and she'd lose her job. Today, my mother is doing great and has lived with bipolar disorder for more than 30 years. She continues on medication, and will for the rest of her life, but she has never been sick again.

Out of one of the most traumatic experiences of my life, my mother, brother and I formed an unbreakable bond. We all still miss my Dad tremendously. I've learned that when you lose someone you love, you learn to live with it, but the pain of loss never really goes away. We talk openly with each other about Mom's illness and the effect that it had on all our lives. Sometimes we even laugh about some of the crazy things she did during that time. I'm blessed that I can look back on events that caused so much pain and find a few moments of joy.

It still amazes me how my life changed so quickly, and as a mother of two young children, I sometimes worry that I won't live to see them grow up. I think of how much our father loved us, and how much he would have wanted to see me graduate from high school and college, get married, and know his grandchildren. It still breaks my heart that we missed that time together.

But some good came from everything I went through. I

developed mental toughness, and there is not too much that gets me down. Plus, I have a high degree of empathy for others who are suffering. And I take nothing for granted. I learned at a young age that you have to make the most of each day. I make every effort to spend as much time with my husband and children as I can. All in all, the adversity I experienced has helped me to live a much richer, fuller life.

Kim Davis recently founded Her Exit Strategy (HerExitStrategy.com), an online community of women focused on supporting women executives who wish to transition from the corporate world to entrepreneurship. She lives in Maryland with her husband and two young children, and is an active member in both her church and community. Kim is also the author of *The Woman's Guide to Creating Balance: 21 Secrets That Will Restore, Re-Energize, and Renew Your Life,* where she shares her personal strategies to help women achieve their goals and bring joy and balance to their lives.

I'M MARRYING ME

*Getting unstuck for the sake of
living authentically*

Beth (Kloesener) Bryce

My job made me miserable—and angry. When I was little and someone asked what I wanted to be when I grew up, I never responded with "accountant." Over the course of my 20-year career, I have found corporate finance to be a world of endless spreadsheets, grueling deadlines, intense pressure, and emails from people who were not fun, namely auditors. Even worse were the emotionally abusive bullies and alcohol and drug addicts I've had to work beside and support.

Eventually my anger evolved into compassion and empathy, but frankly I grew tired of compromising. Stress left me physically ill and emotionally crushed. While the job served me well financially, it created a black hole in my soul. My passion, on the other hand, is career coaching, teaching, and writing. This world consists of mentoring, inspiring and motivating students and professionals to achieve a life of significance. This type of work is my calling and for five years I tried to create a life around it, but my fears paralyzed me.

I realized I was at a breaking point during a pre-dawn visit to a drive-thru for coffee. Reading the latest demands from the auditors on my smartphone, I paid for my coffee and drove off without it. Two miles down the road, I reached for a sip and realized it wasn't there. I've witnessed people do this and thought, "Look at that fool! He just drove off without his food!" Now I was the fool.

I pulled my car to the side of the road and put my head down to collect myself. I thought of Bob Marley's quote, "Love the life you live. Live the life you love." Bob, thank you. I decided it was time to do just that. At the end of the day I rushed home, wrote a resignation letter, and dated it six months from that day. Enough was enough.

NEW YEAR'S DAY

On Dec. 31, 2011, while most people were thinking about parties and a midnight kiss, I was on a different mission. I was in my pajamas working on my annual vision board. I had no idea what my focus would be in 2012. Sadly, the same images and words kept repeating on my board year after year; they remained unanswered.

After a bottle of Moscato and a bag of Doritos, I was fed up with myself and determined to get unstuck. I deserved joy, purpose and passion! I was desperate to find an answer, when my inner voice whispered, "Surround yourself by the mountains, ocean, and desert." These are places where I feel most connected with my spirit. I had to get back to my center to find my authentic self.

I decided to create my own yearlong journey, my own *Eat, Pray, Love* in the United States. Traveling domestically was doable on a Michigan working girl's budget. I hoped to have several Aha! moments, be healthy, and live in alignment with the universe. First I got creative: I dug a fake promotional check out of the junk mail, scratched out where it said "Car Loan" and wrote "Book Advance." Then I pasted it on my vision board as midnight struck. I knew it would be a year unlike any other.

On New Year's Day, I searched the Web for a workshop in one of my targeted spots. I found a writer's workshop in Denver, and one lucky attendee would win a $10,000 book advance and contract. I started making excuses why I shouldn't go. Who would take care of my dog? What if there was a snowstorm? How would I pay for it? In spite of those negative voices, I registered. I had booked my first adventure and checked the mountains off my list.

As I awaited the workshop's April date, I turned my attention to the ocean. I had an unused airline ticket set to expire. Because AirTran didn't fly to Denver, I had to find another use for it. I looked at the list of destinations on their website. The last city was West Palm Beach. I had lived there many years earlier, so it was an obvious choice. I booked my flight.

I reveled in what I had accomplished before noon on New Year's Day!

~ I AM powerful.

"Set your course for Authentica. Legend has it that once you reach her shores, you'll not leave the same woman. For once you find this sacred isle you will remember what you have always known. You will discover the woman you have always been."
~ **Sarah Ban Breathnach,** from *Simple Abundance.*

THE BEACH

It had been 10 years since I last visited south Florida. There is no place I feel more at peace than walking along the beach and listening to the surf. Landing at Palm Beach International in early April, I was giddy with anticipation—the same feeling

I once had arriving there as a college freshman. Cruising I-95 in my rental car, the cityscape was so familiar, as if I had just returned from a long weekend getaway. I drove past old haunts, apartments I had lived in, and the restaurant I had worked in 20 years earlier.

But as I settled into my hotel bed, I panicked. How could I stay four days here alone? What was I thinking? Unable to sleep, I dialed the airline, prepared to move up my departure date. Then I realized that I was afraid of reliving my past. I had work to do, letting go of past hurts so I could welcome in the future.

The days that followed included trips down memory lane, visiting old girlfriends and eating at favorite cafes, but I saved the best for last, the beach. It was a beautiful day, and the smell and sound of the ocean embraced me. I intended to read and soak in the sun, but mysteriously I felt guided elsewhere. As I walked along the beach, I picked up rocks. Two hours later, I faced the waves crashing in. With salt on my face—from the sea and my tears—I named each stone, said a forgiveness prayer and tossed it back into the waves. Then I watched as the sea washed away all my past hurts and troubles.

Afterward, I sat on the beach and wrote vows to myself: I promised to love, cherish, and honor myself; to never give up on my dreams, or to settle for less than I deserve. I raised my face and the sun kissed my eyes, my cheeks, and my lips. I committed to living a life on purpose, authentically and with my whole heart. As I looked out over the water it seemed the sound of the thunderous waves pounding in was actually applause—even the ocean was celebrating my accomplishment!

Four days later, I boarded the plane with a liberated spirit. At home, a small box had arrived in the mail. A huge grin swept across my face as I ripped open the package. It was a ring I had ordered before the trip, a beautiful antique silver band and 1.25 carats of Absolute™ diamond. It cost $19.95, but on my ring finger, it was priceless.

~ I AM worthy.

"Be not troubled, for the beach is close at hand. You need only to deliver your strife to the tranquility of the beach and it shall be exercised from you." ~ **Poet Joe Fazio,** from "Under a Blanket of Stars."

THE MOUNTAINS

The plane landed in Denver after circling for almost an hour because of the small matter of a tornado touchdown. Despite darkness and pouring rain, I made it safely to my hotel room where I threw open the blinds. Already I felt exhilarated by the twinkling lights of the tall buildings. It was late April. Before the writer's workshop began, I had a day I decided to use to drive north through Boulder to Estes Park.

In Boulder I meandered through small boutiques. I entered a store with exquisite handcrafted jewelry from local artists. I gasped like a kid in a candy store. A soft voice said, "Isn't their jewelry amazing?" I exclaimed, "Oh, yes!" The shop owner put down her tools and opened case after case, pointing out several pieces. She asked where I was from and why I was there. I told her I came to Denver for a writer's workshop. "Oh my!" she said. "You're a writer!" Rather than respond that I worked in accounting, I paused. Suddenly it washed over me: I am a writer. "Yes, I am!" I responded. I was giddy as I described my book idea to her. She was intrigued and excited for me. As I waved goodbye, I made a mental note to send her a signed copy of my first book.

From that moment on, I was no longer an accountant who likes to write, but rather a writer who can count. The fact that the workshop started by informing us that 85 percent of writers never finish a book proposal didn't mean a thing to me. I went there to learn how to put together a book proposal, but I discovered something far more valuable. It wasn't about knowing how to write; it was about believing that I am a writer.

Back home, a dear friend told me I needed to create a writing space. She said it's most important to have a place that comforts, supports, and inspires you. My den is cozy, with a huge bay window capturing the morning sunrise. I placed my desk in front of it. I proudly told myself: "Here is where I will create my best-selling book, listen to smooth jazz, and sip dark roast coffee." It was a new day.

~ I AM a writer.

"Coming home to a place he'd never been before / He left yesterday behind him / You might say he was born again / You might say he found a key for every door" ~ **Singer John Denver,** from "Rocky Mountain High."

THE SABBATICAL

Since this was my year of change, I made another huge decision, this time concerning my health. I wanted to finally end my long battle with uterine fibroid tumors. I scheduled myself for a hysterectomy, a surgery I had put off for four years. I had tried every other alternative course: changing my diet, acupuncture, hormones, smaller surgeries, and even intravenously taking iron to ward off my severe anemia. When it got to the point of my possibly needing a blood transfusion I was forced to finally ask: Why am I punishing myself? What are my fears?

When my problems started, I wasn't yet 40. I considered having a child, but kept putting it off, fretting that the busyness of corporate climbing and travel didn't provide much time to start a family. I was trying to save my uterus in case I wanted a child. But did I? I never dreamt of having a family; I had no visions of children playing, first days of school, sporting events or holiday traditions. While I like children, I didn't want the responsibility of having my own. That doesn't make me less of a woman, nor does it make me a bad person. When I came to terms with the fact that having children wasn't for me, the decision to have the surgery was a no-brainer. It was such a relief, emotionally as well as physically.

The surgery took place in May. I was up and about only days later. Over the six weeks of recovery, I took naps with my dog, walked outdoors, read, worked on my book, and got stronger. My energy came back, and I was stronger in body and mind than I'd been in a long time. I even started rollerblading again after an 18-year hiatus.

While the stress lines vanished from my face, I dreaded going back to my accounting job. I didn't want my old life; I had outgrown it. When I did go back, in my mind, it was only temporary. It was time to move forward with my dreams.

~ I AM healthy.

"Are you a princess? I said. And she said I'm much more than a princess but you don't have a name for it yet here on earth."
~ **Artisan and storyteller Brian Andreas,** from *Story People*

THE DESERT

At my 45th birthday party in August I blew out the candles on my cake and wished for the courage to leave my job. Less than a week later, my wish came true. The pain of staying finally outweighed the pain of leaving. Like any bad relationship, we both knew I had been there way too long and it was time for me go.

On my last day, I quietly packed what few belongings I had stashed in a filing cabinet. Truthfully, I had been packing for months, gradually taking home pictures, a coffeemaker, a small refrigerator, and even my framed college degree. I drove home with a Cheshire cat grin and free spirit, never looking back. Not knowing what the future held didn't matter. I was free. Free from a job and work environment that was sucking the life out of me. Free to pursue my dreams and live a life of purpose and passion. I was so free that I went home and spent a summer afternoon rollerblading without a care in the world.

In search of a spiritual cleansing, I read a description of a spa treatment for a "turquoise wrap" in a place called Carefree, Arizona. I couldn't dial the phone fast enough! Turquoise is not only one of the most vibrant colors of the desert, but there is also a Native American belief that it is a color of protection, self-confidence, and positive energy. Two weeks later, in September, my mom and I were on a plane headed to Phoenix. Both of us, dealing with grief after my grandfather's passing, longed for healing and serenity. Surely, the desert would guide us to it.

There is an indescribable strength being in the desert, surrounded by boulders thousands of years old, even in a spa robe sipping herbal tea. As I soaked up the Hopi blue-clay wrap and its skin-purifying benefits, my masseuse performed a spiritual cleansing "rain stick ritual" with traditional essential oils. After each layer, she gave me a warm shower, compassionately tending to my inner wounds. Stresses, hurts, and self-doubts were left behind in the puddles on the spa room floor. Afterward, walking through a Zen meditation garden, spiritually renewed, I chuckled when a baby bunny greeted me. Zuni Indians believe rabbits represent transcending your fears and are also a sign of fertility. With a deep sigh, I acknowledged that it was indeed time to birth the "new" me.

Back home that October, I turned in my leased car. The salesman filling out a new lease application asked what we should put for my new occupation. Teacher? I agreed. Right at that moment, my email notification went off. It was a welcome letter from a local community college where, back in March, I had applied to teach classes. The email started with, "Welcome, Professor." The salesman and I hugged each other and our cries of joy filled the dealership. It was official!

~ I AM a teacher.

> *"Everything on the earth has a purpose, every disease an herb to cure it, and every person a mission. This is the Indian theory of existence."* ~ **Mourning Dove (Christine Quintasket, Native American writer, 1888-1936)**

YEAR END

To celebrate my extraordinary year, I wanted to do something spectacular and meaningful. For a long time I had been struggling over the decision to change my last name. My current surname, as I've been told by hundreds of strangers, friends, co-workers, and clients, is hard to spell, pronounce and Google. Rather than attract opportunities into my life, it does the opposite. My intuition tells me part of my rebirth includes a new last name. The girly girl in me says it's a necessary part of marrying me. Also, both my mom and aunt experienced empowerment from changing their surnames during periods of transition. They still speak of it with words like liberation, confidence, and self-renewal. I decided it finally felt right for me to follow their example. After researching name meanings, I found one that sang to me: Bryce. A numerology report confirmed everything my intuition told me: Bryce adds joy, inspiration, creativity, and stimulates enthusiasm and excitement.

And so…Beth Bryce married herself on a sunny day at the beach, in a jewelry store nestled in the Rockies, on an operating table, and in a Zen meditation garden in the desert. Now it was all about planning the wedding announcement on my official court date and, of course, the party!

Over this one year, I experienced an incredible journey to live authentically. And the story is far from over. It seems fitting that "Wonder" is my theme for 2013. I have no expectations other than I will be in constant awe of how my life unfolds.

Today I face new opportunities and a tough decision between career coaching in academia or leadership coaching in the corporate world. For a few years, my vision has been to work at a university; now I'm not sure if that's big enough for me. After grappling with uncertainty, I remind myself that sometimes, on the way to a dream, you get lost and find a better one.

While I struggle to determine my "next best chapter," I know the answer lies in trusting myself and listening to my intuition. The following is a letter from my journal, one of many I've written in times of self-doubt and change:

Dear Beth,

You are brilliant, talented, compassionate, kind and capable. Never forget this. Hope and faith overcome fear. If you didn't believe in yourself you would have never made it this far. Every move has led you to a brighter tomorrow. You must believe in yourself! You have plenty of time to recreate a life of passion and purpose, but tomorrow is promised to no one. Here you are at a crossroad, where you have been so many times before and made the right decision. Believe you will figure this out too. I know you can live authentically.

Beth

So 366 days later, I am pleased to announce:

- I AM the healthiest I've been in years.
- I AM a coach, writer, teacher.
- I AM living authentically.

And you can too.

"Somewhere at the intersection of joy, fear and mystery and insight lies awe, that ineffable response to the amazing world around us." ~ **David Hochman,** from *The Key to Fulfillment*

Beth Bryce is a certified motivational career coach and founder of Girls2Women Coaching—a career coaching firm that helps students and professional women to define a rewarding career path for their authentic self to obtain personal growth, whole-hearted success and financial independence. She enjoys jogging through the occasional marathon, inspiring others to marry themselves, and traveling the world searching for the best food, the best spas, and life-changing adventures. Visit her websites at www.girls2womencoaching.com and www.bethbryce.com.

PART TWO: STRATEGIES

PUSHED BACK TO SQUARE ONE

Re-building a life, block by block

Leah Hamilton

It had been an enjoyable three-day weekend, a chance to relax after a tough semester. On the last afternoon, my best girlfriend and I stopped by a coffee shop. There, I met Dave (not his real name). We talked over a latte before he asked me out for a beer chaser. After drinks, he took me home to meet his puppy. Then we shared a bottle of chardonnay and fell in love.

I was content with my life at the time—working full time in the arts, going to grad school, teaching art to children, and exhibiting my own artwork. I was independent and my life seemed to be flowing according to plan. Still, I moved in with Dave three weeks later.

He was the man of my dreams—creative, cute, funny, caring. He was also an entrepreneur, his own man. His photography business was thriving. Our lives meshed together well. I earned my master's degree and began work at the Illinois Arts Council. I helped him; he helped me. He bought a 12,000-sq.ft. building on the West side of Chicago and converted part of it into a two-bedroom loft; it also doubled as his studio and workplace. Our lives moved at a quick clip, and we pushed our type-A selves to achieve. We were inspired and in love.

We had dated for five years when he stole me away to Barbados to propose. We married on Memorial Day in 1998 when I was 30 years old.

One year later, I delivered our son, Max. I quit my job to become a full-time mom. This had been my dream, and we were fortunate that we could get by on Dave's income. With my background in arts-in-education, I knew that exposing children to art, dance, music, and drama at an early age was important, and it was what Dave and I wanted for our children.

It was a glorious time. Everything was brand new and wonderful—our marriage, our home, our baby. Two years later, I was pregnant again.

MOVING UP AND ON

With a second child on the way, we bought a stunning, three-story Victorian home on the North side. But I didn't really want to move. I liked loft living and didn't want the burden of a yard or an old house that would need constant fixing. Still, I found myself in charge of packing and organizing our relocation.

The day we closed on the house was also my due date, but I had been nine days late with Max, so I figured I would have a similar experience this time. After the closing, I ran to the store to prepare for an open house at our new home that evening for 30 people.

Back at the house, I was up and down the stairs to the third floor, answering questions for Dave, who was engrossed in plans for a renovation. By the time the gathering broke up that evening,

I was exhausted, but Dave was ready to start ripping out the kitchen wall.

At 1 a.m., I was in labor, and Olivia was in my arms at 6:40 a.m. Almost immediately, Dave kissed me and the baby, said "Love you," and was off to the new home to tear down that wall.

We all went back to the loft the next day. Over the next weeks, I nursed the baby, packed for the move, strolled to the park, played with the children, and found peace in the bathtub during the 20 minutes their naps overlapped. Dave made the rounds between the loft, work, and the new house. When we moved into the big house two months later, I felt completely isolated and thought I had the "baby blues." Now I know it was much deeper than that.

During the transition from the loft to the house, I was spread thin, caring for an infant and a toddler, plus there was a blur of decisions to be made. I was home alone nursing and couldn't leave for more than two hours at a stretch. I didn't want to burden my family and friends or give the impression that I was weak or needy. I had a perfectionist quality that kept me from reaching out and asking for help. From a young age, I had learned to hide my feelings and vulnerabilities, and Dave came from a similar background. Neither of us was well versed in conflict resolution.

Dave was always too busy to take my calls, and when we did talk, I felt like a nuisance interrupting his important life. It was assumed that I would manage all the day-to-day operations, and he didn't want to hear complaining or venting. In his mind, I was living the easy life, with carte blanche on the credit cards, throwing lavish parties and going on magical vacations. But I was deeply sad and alone. Dave was making interesting new friends through his work circles. It made me miss my interaction with co-workers and friends.

I began having mixed feelings about having given up my career, but I didn't see a way to integrate work back into my life. I wanted to be there with my children, but I also wanted my own thing. I started to take my pulse: I realized that I needed to grow.

Dave and I decided to go into counseling. During an early session, the therapist drew a small circle and identified it as my life; then she drew a big circle identified as Dave's life. The crossover was a thin line. I could not believe I'd let my world get so small. I was angry with myself.

Then there was an incident that really woke me up. I was going to meet Dave, his rep, and some clients for dinner. I rushed the kids home after school, made them a snack, set up the homework situation, jumped in the shower, and confirmed the babysitter. The kids needed my constant attention as I tried to blow out my hair, do my makeup, and dress. Finally, I raced to make it to the other side of town on time.

I waited at the bar, expecting the entourage to enter at any moment. After about 15 minutes I ordered a glass of wine. An hour went by. There was no call, no text, no consideration of my time and efforts to be supportive.

Finally, the group walked in and Dave introduced me, but there was no hug, no apology for keeping me waiting, no "thanks for coming." I felt like a tag-along. I was hurt and disappointed. I drove home alone in my car, thinking about how Dave's clients always came first and foremost, even before the family. He was a workaholic, obsessed with his career. It had gotten worse since he turned 40; he went from being confident to scared of losing everything.

Dave came in a half-hour behind me, and I said that we needed to talk. I told him I was tired of being the bottom of the barrel, unacknowledged and unappreciated. His response was direct: "Get a life and stay out of mine."

BABY STEPS TO REDISCOVERY

Shocked and heartbroken, I relived the moment with my therapist. She agreed that I needed my own friends, work, and support to return my focus back onto me. I thought being a dedicated wife and mother was enough, but deep down I knew I had lost myself. I had to get my power back. I felt pressure to be the perfect mom and wife, yet I knew I needed to put my oxygen mask on and save myself.

Just carrying a normal workload had never been good enough for me. I constantly sought approval and affirmation because I didn't know what "normal" was. I tried to figure it out from the actions and reactions of others. Growing up with an alcoholic father had left me absolutely terrified of abandonment. It kept me holding on to an unhealthy relationship with Dave.

I took baby steps forward in my journey to rediscover myself. I had an idea to write a guidebook called *Around the World with Your Kids in Chicago,* focusing on international family experiences in my amazing city, and I needed advice to get started. I saw a listing for a workshop about writing a purpose statement and registered. I was the only one who showed up for the workshop that rainy night. Then I learned that the topic of the class was on writing a PERSONAL purpose statement. It turned out to be just what I needed. Even better, I met life coach Hallie Crawford.

We took advantage of the one-on-one time, and Hallie did a visualization exercise with me that I will never forget. I closed my eyes and she guided me through questions about my future self. I imagined myself 25 years older, my gray hair in a ponytail, dressed in a black flowing dress, surrounded by art. The doorbell rang, Hallie told me, so in my mind, I opened the door. My current self was standing there. We sat down and had a conversation. My older self gave my current self advice, courage, strength, and vision. She told me to take care of myself and trust my instincts. This was a welcomed epiphany.

Blown away by the insights, I knew I'd found the right coach for me, one who touched my soul, who understood me, and could support and help me. I left that evening with my purpose statement and a renewed commitment. I worked with Hallie for a year and a half on fulfilling myself as a wife and mother. We continually asked "What is next?" and "How can I be better? Not only for me, but also for those around me."

Around the World with Your Kids in Chicago was family focused and revolved around my values, but I needed something just for me. My new perspective helped me to see that I was feeling many conflicting societal pressures and expectations. I needed to let go of the old ideals. I realized that women go through phases as wives and mothers; we may lose ourselves but then something happens that brings us back. I was slowly inching back to myself. I started oil painting more and volunteering at my children's school, specifically on larger art-related projects. I spearheaded a cookbook, joke book, dream portraits, and hand portraits, to name a few initiatives. But one changed me forever.

Max's first grade teacher was pregnant, and what a joy it was for her and our school community. Several of us parents jumped at the opportunity to throw a baby shower for her. We thought it would be meaningful if each child made something special for the baby. Since she was a teacher who loved creative expression, I thought she would adore personalized wooden blocks designed by each of the students. On a beautiful day, we sat on the playground on giant, colorful parachutes, and the kids made blocks for the baby-to-be. The adorable 6- and 7-year-olds created brightly colored patterns—such as ABCs, 123s, animals, symbols, silly faces, and messages like "Welcome to the world!"—all in one big box with a bow. It was a beautiful, heartfelt gift.

After the shower, I received requests for kits. I started to think this was an undiscovered niche, and I got serious about how to put it together. I told my brother, a brilliant engineer, that I wanted to use bamboo rather than maple for my toy because it is eco-friendly. He assured me this would be simple to achieve. I hired a designer and a marketing team to help me research and create a business and product identity. I held focus groups. One step at a time, I created a product and a company. Belly Productions was born, and Be Blocks was on the production line in China.

I became an entrepreneur. I was fortunate to have had firsthand experience witnessing Dave build his business. I had seen the challenges of day-to-day operations. He was a talented businessman who liked his work and had skillful support systems. I wanted that too. Starting my own business was empowering. I had a renewed sense of purpose; I felt challenged and inspired again.

PUSHING THROUGH THE FEAR

I was motivated and excited, but I was also frightened. I would easily become overwhelmed by the size and scope of the process. When life became emotionally painful, I would sleep instead of push myself.

I decided to be gentle with my feelings and compassionate about my process. I often needed to remind myself that I am a human being doing my best each day. It does not have to happen all at once; I can reflect, breathe, and think. I would replay my day in my mind before bed and meditate to Marianne Williamson to calm my mind, stop the worrying, and focus on the positive. Some days, just making it through the day without crying was an achievement. Other days, I would come home from working out, put on loud music, brew a pot of coffee, eat chocolate-covered almonds, and just get stuff done. In the mornings, I would often think of Sylvester Stallone's character

Rocky Balboa and hum the song "Eye of the Tiger." I had a picture of Rocky over my bed to remind me that I could do it.

It was hard work and quite a juggle, but I was equipped to multitask. Besides the issues with Dave, I was also now dealing with my brother as a businessperson, which was a new family dynamic. I had manufacturers, vendors, accountants, lawyers, designers, and business development sessions. I jumped on the roller coaster and had no idea the ride was going to be so fun, fast, and ferocious.

I set a goal to take Be Blocks to the New York City Toy Fair, and I made it. The show was amazing. Dave and my kids came with me to New York City a couple days early, and we saw the sites, including going to Chinatown to buy lucky bamboo. I was so excited to set up my 10-by-10-foot booth. It looked professional, approachable, and creative, with a big, beautiful banner, a colorful video running, order forms, business cards, block samples, and lots of heavy, gorgeous product.

To my astonishment I received a "WOW" response and was voted one of the top 10 toys of the New York City Toy Fair by *Toy Directory Monthly* and featured in their publication. I was interviewed and featured in *Daily Candy Kids Chicago*. I was thrilled, but it would be a long time before I could stop and smell the roses. I had orders to fulfill!

Dave called Be Blocks a project, and I called it a business. I was sitting at my computer checking my email when I saw the *Daily Candy Kids Chicago* email blast. When I screamed to Dave that Be Blocks was just featured, his reply was, "I spend $50,000 a year in marketing and advertising, and you get it for free." No congratulations.

What a bittersweet moment. I was thrilled for me, yet I saw that my husband was not on my side. Instead, he was competing with me. I had thought he wanted the best for me because he wanted the best for us. Clearly, he was more concerned about himself.

Then he told me to start figuring out my credit and finances.

Since he was in control of our financial lives, I again was taken aback. But I started building my own credit. The writing was on the wall, and I had to seriously prepare.

Still, when Dave finally did leave me and file for divorce, I was on the floor for weeks. I felt frightened, abandoned, and alone. I thought I would not be able to make it without him. Eventually, I realized that I was still standing; I *was* making it. I got up and wiped away my tears. I needed to be strong for my beautiful children and for myself. The desire to regain myself, to strengthen myself was now not just a desire but also a requirement.

I had a huge support system of family, friends, colleagues, staff, a therapist, a life coach, physical trainers, and the best legal team in the United States. Most important, I had myself. I started dating again and found it fascinating and fun. I now have a big circle, and it grows each day. I am carrying the torch for my family and it's so wild that life has really come full circle. I wear a circle pendant around my neck to remind me of this journey and my big sparkly circle, which all started with focusing on me.

I have new dreams now based on me and what I want and who I am. With my new perspective, tools, and strength, my dreams are to have a peaceful home, happy children, and a loving, multidimensional partner. I want to expand Belly Productions by creating an entire line, including Be Blocks, Be Beads, Be Books, Be Bags, specialized stencil sets for baby showers and more and then sell the business. I want to wake up to watch the sun rising over the water from my bed and end my day drinking a glass of wine with my love as we watch the sunset. I want to go to Machu Picchu, Argentina, and Australia, to live to be 101 years old and have a dance party to celebrate. I want to inspire and connect people, to deepen my relationships and meditate more.

My journey is about redefining my dreams, not shifting them from family to me, but allowing them to expand. I am redefining myself as a mother. I know myself better than I ever have, and

I am able to give more through love, support, and empowering others and myself. I have learned that when I am realizing my dreams, all of our worlds are better. Opening my heart to others allows me to be more open to myself and invites opportunity. I am reaching for my whole person and doing it for me. I am nourishing my heart as well as others, and always listening to my inner voice.

It has been an incredible journey and looking back I would not skip a single step. I am still growing and, clearly, I did get a life.

Entrepreneur **Leah Hamilton** established Belly Productions Inc. in 2009, a company committed to creativity and environmental consciousness among kids, parents, and gift-givers. Producing Be Blocks and founding Belly Productions culminate Hamilton's lifelong artistic experiences and activities. She earned a B.A. from Cornell College and a master's in arts management from Columbia College in Chicago. She worked at arts and education organizations Gallery 37, Urban Gateways, and Illinois Arts Council. Leah resides in the Chicago historical landmark neighborhood Lakewood/Balmoral. In 2001 she rehabbed her 1899 Victorian home where she lives with her two children.

SCALING NEW HEIGHTS

A mother conquers her phobia to become a better parent

Carrie Saba

"Courage is very important. Like a muscle, it is strengthened by use." **–Ruth Gordon**

I've always had an I-can-do-it attitude, even as a child—at least that's what I've been told by my family. When I face challenging times, a little voice inside cheers me on: "You can do it! You can get through this!" This approach to life demands both a willingness to prepare and perseverance—two attributes I have in abundance. So with these traits as part of my foundation, I was completely taken aback in my early 20s to discover that I had a paralyzing phobia against which my strengths were useless.

It was a fear of heights. Caught in the wrong place, at the wrong altitude, I would freeze. My heart would pound so loudly that it sounded like it was coming from a source outside my body. Tears would stream down my face, but I couldn't wipe them away. I could barely breathe. There was no inner voice cheering me on.

Fear overtook every part of me.

But this fear crept quietly into my life. I'm not even sure where it began and once it appeared, I never spoke about it. I tried to ignore it. Then a moment would arise where I'd find myself a little too high, looking down a little too far and—bam!—there it was again.

This was not a problem I had when I was a kid. I know this because I remember going to an amusement park when I was probably 8 to 10 years old. I went up the replica of the Eiffel Tower, which, while only one-third the size of the real Eiffel Tower, was still pretty high. And I loved it! I remember being so excited that I could see the entire park. It felt freeing. But somewhere between childhood and adulthood, things began to change.

I remember one vivid moment, the first undeniable sign of a deep fear. It was during a skiing trip to Lake Tahoe in 1992. I was a senior in college, and I had lived and worked there the summer before. I loved it so much, and I wanted to revisit the area in winter. And the thing to do in the winter at Lake Tahoe is ski. I had skied only twice before—on the hills of Ohio, which are nothing compared to the mountains of Lake Tahoe. While riding the ski lift, I could feel my body tense, but I didn't yet accept its message of fear. I got off the lift and watched my friends take off down the trail. As I started after them, I was struck by the vast view of the lake—and with how really far up I was. I panicked. I fell to the ground and could not move. A stream of protests raced through my mind: "I'm not going down! I'm not doing this!"

A friend realized I had fallen and yelled encouragements up to me before heading off in search of the ski patrol. I began to slide down the mountain on my butt—about a foot at a time. I felt so alone and thought, "What if I'm stuck up here by myself when it gets dark?" I finally made it to an area that was flat and waited for help to arrive. It was such a relief to finish the descent on a snow mobile. I came to the conclusion that I was not a skier. I thought skiing was the problem and didn't consider that it really was the elevation that had terrified me.

AN UNAVOIDABLE CONCLUSION

A few years later, I went to Paris with my boyfriend (and now husband), Stephan. We did all of the touristy sightseeing, which of course included the Eiffel Tower. I was especially excited to go there because of my wonderful memories of the replica I visited as a child.

There are two stops where you can walk around on the way up to the upper observation deck. I was thrilled to be going up the Eiffel Tower, so I was oblivious to what was about to happen to me as I stepped out of the elevator at the first level, about a quarter of the way up. I gazed out and down, all the way to the street. I instantly froze. My feet felt like they were encased in concrete; my knees turned to JELL-O. Standing was no longer an option. I basically scrunched down to the metal flooring, which you could see through, and inched my way to the side.

I sat in a fetal position and tried to pull myself together the best I could. I encouraged Stephan to go to the top, saying I would stay where I was. I hugged my knees to my chest, awaiting his return. Then he had to help me stand and held me while we crept to the elevator. I remember thinking, "I might be scared of heights." Memories came flooding back of other times I had felt a similar sensation while up high. I was actually shocked by this sudden revelation. But from that point forward, I avoided situations where my fear could take over. I had no idea how I would ever overcome it, or if I even wanted to try.

For years I did a good job of keeping my fear stuffed down

inside. I learned how not to let myself get into a position that would bring on the terror. But then my strategy hit a snag: I became the mother of two daughters, Skylar in 1999 and Callie in 2002.

One thing Stephan and I absolutely wanted to do with our daughters was travel. We loved it and wanted to instill that passion in them. When it was only the two of us, we had been able to travel without compromising my desire to avoid high places. But when we started to go on trips with our children, I worried that the girls could miss out on something special because of my phobia. And I did not want my fear to be transferred to them. If they wanted to climb stairs in historical places or go to famous tourist locations with an elevated view, I wanted them to experience it positively.

With the support of Stephan, we figured out a way in which I could go with them to such locations, but he would be in charge of the girls. I would stand far away from any high ledges or outlook points. This approach worked well for many years, and I could go up to high places and never have a panic attack. In fact, I started to forget that I had a fear of heights or maybe I thought I had overcome it.

But then my over-confidence caused a setback. I had ignored and "managed" my phobia for so long it hadn't crossed my mind that, if I were alone with my children, it could suddenly take over, potentially putting their safety at risk. Until it happened.

We were in Chicago, and I was on an outing with Skylar and Callie, without Stephan. We went to the top of a tall building, and the girls walked toward the railing to look out. I went with them. Even though there was fencing, the ability to see to the ground took my breath. All of a sudden, panic washed over me. I could not move my feet. I managed to extend my arms, and the girls held onto me. That was all I could do, but keeping them safe trumped my fear of heights just enough for me to tell them in a calm, strong voice to move away from the edge. At first, they were their curious selves and didn't want to back up. I said it again a little stronger, still frozen in place. Once they moved away from the railing, I took a deep breath and told them we needed to go. They listened.

TIME FOR CHANGE

One of my primary jobs as a mother is keeping my children safe, and in that moment, I did not feel capable of performing my duty. I had not had a full-out panic attack, as I had in the past, but my fear was strong enough to make me feel that I was not in complete control. My responses were limited. I was furious with myself for thinking I could take them to such a place without Stephan. My disappointment and anger toward myself drove me to the point of knowing that I needed to make a change. I didn't know what I was going to do, but regaining control became of critical importance, for my children's sake.

I believe that we are often divinely guided, that God gives us signs to follow. It is then up to us to recognize and accept the lessons before us. Not long after I decided I needed to tackle my fear head on, I was helping a friend with travel plans and came across information on Miraval Resort and Spa in Tucson, Arizona, one of Oprah's favorite spas. I read every word of the brochure. It spoke to me. When I saw they had "challenge" activities, I immediately thought that could be helpful in facing my fear of heights. I had a strong gut feeling that I would indeed go there one day.

A few days later, a friend recommended a book by spiritual teacher Sonia Choquette. I was intrigued by her teachings and wanted to learn more about her. As those thoughts crossed my mind, I saw a shooting star. Shooting stars have been significant in my life, and when they show up, I pay attention to what I'm thinking about at the time. I went to Sonia's website to see what workshops she offered. I could not believe what I saw: She was presenting a seminar at Miraval Resort and Spa! My jaw dropped as I moved closer to my computer to be sure I was seeing things correctly. My entire body had goose bumps, and I knew this was another sign.

I shared the story with my mom, leaving out the part about my phobia. She decided she would go with me. We had never gone on a trip together without other family members, and I was surprised and excited that she had an interest in going with me. We arrived in Miraval on Nov. 3, 2005, and settled in. Mom was skeptical about the classes with Sonia, but agreed to go to the first session and see what it was about. I had not shared with her why I wanted to do the challenge activities, only that I was going to sign up for two of them. She decided she would also try one.

Both of the exercises I participated in involved high elevations, but I was secured to a harness, which put my mind at ease a little. The first activity was to climb a pole and walk across a log suspended 30 feet in the air and then to fall backward. The second one was climbing a 25-foot pole, standing on top of it and then jumping off. The focus was on trust. I was nervous but in a good way.

The staff was encouraging and supportive. I shared with them that I had a fear of heights and that this was part of my journey to begin healing. Before and during both activities, I envisioned myself completing them and being safe. I continually said affirmations as I climbed: "I can do this. I am safe." This helped keep fearful and negative thoughts from taking over my mind. I also prayed, specifically The Lord's Prayer, particularly when I was gearing up to jump or fall backward. I surrendered to my faith and I believed I would be safe.

I was able to complete both activities without freezing up or freaking out. I was so proud of myself and happy my mom was with me. She attempted one of the activities, but pain in her hands kept her from completing it. She cheered me on from below, and

I could feel her love and support. I took a giant leap that day in overcoming my fears, and the classes with Sonia had a positive impact on both my mom and me on a deeply spiritual level.

BACK ON THE SLOPES

The following year, Skylar and Callie gave me a challenge, or I should say, a dose of my own medicine. They said, "Mom, we think you need to try skiing. You always want us to try new things. Maybe you can take a lesson. We want you to ski with us."

They had been skiing for a few years with Stephan, and I was content to watch them from the bottom of the hill or mountain. I explained to them that I had tried it before they were born and it didn't work for me. But, as they continued to persuade me, I thought I would give it a try. And since I was working toward overcoming my acrophobia, I agreed to take a lesson. Skylar and Callie were so excited, and that gave me the confidence to take another step forward.

After a few lessons, I started out on very easy slopes. As I practiced, I worked my way up to trying the medium runs. The positive support I got from my girls kept me wanting to try harder. I would focus internally and visualize myself making it down the slopes without an incident of fear taking over.

I was doing so well with skiing, often at higher altitudes, that I started to believe I had conquered my fear. But then an incident in icy conditions set me back. Stephan and Skylar were already down the slope, and Callie was close by me. We approached a steep section that looked like a sheet of ice. I came to a stop, afraid to go any further. I looked down the run and saw that we were high up. I could feel my heart pounding as fear started to take over. Callie noticed I had stopped and was waiting for me.

I gripped my poles, not knowing what to do. I was grateful

for my goggles so Callie couldn't see I was crying. She encouraged me and waited patiently while I moved a foot or two forward and then had to stop again to regroup. She told me to say a prayer. She coached me, giving me the strength and courage I needed to continue. I will never forget her words of love and comfort. It makes me cry to think about it.

OVER THE EDGE

For several years, I continued to take every opportunity to step outside my comfort zone: challenging ski runs, roller coasters— with my eyes open! I was really letting go of my fear. I had an idea that if I could get on *The Amazing Race,* the reality show that teams contestants in a race around the world with challenges along the way, it would be proof that I had indeed overcome my fear. I auditioned and applied three times but never made it on the show.

My dad knew how much I loved *The Amazing Race,* and he had heard about a fundraiser called "Over the Edge for Kids' Sake," benefiting Big Brothers Big Sisters of Central Ohio taking place on Oct. 12, 2012. It included rappelling off the 20th floor of the PNC Bank building in downtown Columbus. This reminded Dad of a challenge that would be on the show, and because I had worked for Big Brothers Big Sisters of Broward County when I lived in Florida, he thought I might be interested in doing it with him. I immediately said yes and began fundraising efforts to get enough money to participate. We called our team Courage for Kids.

One of my dad's friends, who was making a donation to support us, shared how there was no way he could participate in the event because he was afraid of heights. I thought, "I used to be scared of heights too." *Used to be.* I realized that I wasn't afraid to take on the challenge. In fact, fear never crossed my mind. Could it be that I had actually overcome it? The resounding answer from within was YES!

While I know I took a little longer going over the edge than most did that day, I smiled almost the entire way down. My dad was rappelling right beside me, and I was able to talk to him. I could breathe; I could move my body. And I made it to the bottom without feeling petrified. I had fun and felt so alive. My fear was gone, and it left as quietly as it had come into my life.

Had I not had that experience with my girls on top of the building I might never have begun my process of chipping away at my phobia and would have missed out on some amazing experiences. And I would have continued to let fear have a hold on me.

It took years for me to move past my fears, but I did it through commitment and taking baby steps forward. I found it was unhealthy to keep the phobia a secret. By sharing it with those who love me and asking for their support, I began to face it. The encouragement I received from my family helped me through some very challenging times. Another strategy that helped me was to crowd out my negative self-talk with positive thoughts that I *could* do it. I visualized accomplishing a task while smiling and feeling good.

There were setbacks, but that was okay. I simply tried again. I found strength in prayer and in keeping the faith that I could overcome the fear. I believed it was possible.

Having courage for my kids has given me many joys in life I could have missed. I hope that someday my daughters realize how big of a role they played in helping me let go of a fear that once crippled me. I am forever grateful.

Carrie Saba is a health and lifestyle coach. She is an open-hearted listener of your truth, a passionate believer in loving yourself and a fun-seeking nature lover. Her intuitive and upbeat coaching style creates a safe space where she will meet you where you are and support you as you move closer to where you want to be. Carrie graduated with a B.A. from The Ohio University and received her coaching certification from The Institute for Integrative Nutrition. She is also certified through The American Association of Drugless Practitioners. Carrie helps you discover simple and effective techniques to start making you a priority in your own life, so you are living a life you love. Visit www.CarrieSaba.com

HIS, HERS, AND OURS

Successful co-parenting by design

Maria Verroye

It's funny, but I can't remember specifically sitting down with Pierre to discuss co-parenting, beyond basic logistics. Prior to our divorce, we were both really solid in our mutual support. We agreed on rules and boundaries as well as the big-picture ideas about the kind of people we wanted our daughters to be—good, kind, and decent. And that alliance carried over into our divorce, although it wasn't always easy. Even during emotionally challenging times, we held on to the notion that we had to find a way to work together.

I met Pierre in 1982 when we were attending Juniata College in Huntingdon, Pennsylvania. He was a French exchange student, and we met on the soccer field when I tried out for the boys' team; there wasn't one for girls. He and others disagreed with my being cut from the team—due to the "complications" of having a girl as a player—and he presented me with his soccer letter at the end of the year with a card saying that I should've made the team.

The exchange led to our becoming pen pals when he returned to France. I visited him when I studied in England during my junior year, and we became engaged. A year later, we were married. We really didn't know each other, but we blissfully romanticized our relationship.

We started a family almost immediately. Then, to add to our stress, we moved to France with our two young children and lived with his parents. I was depressed and sullen; Pierre was disengaged, frustrated with our lack of communication, and struggling to find a job.

After giving our "trial year" about five months, we moved back to the United States, but by 1992 our marriage was crumbling. So, naturally, we had another baby! This, of course, didn't solve any of our problems, and finally, we agreed to divorce when our girls—Natasha, Juliette, and Chloe—were 7, 6, and 2 years old. According to Maryland law, we had to live separately for a year before the divorce could be finalized. Since I had initiated the divorce (and felt guilty), I decided I should be the one to bite the bullet, so I moved into a friend's house. I continued to spend days with the children in "our" home. I'd arrive by 7 a.m., before anyone else was awake, and do the stay-at-home-mom drill, which I'd been doing since our oldest, Natasha, was born. Then I'd tuck everyone into bed at night, pack a bag and head across town.

When the divorce was final, I moved into an apartment about two miles from Pierre's house and began a job flexible enough to allow me to be what I called a "pretend stay-at-home mom," meaning I could fit chauffeuring the kids to school, childcare, doctor appointments, and all their other activities into my work schedule, and also be home when school was out. Pierre and I began a shared parenting arrangement in which the children spent weekdays with me and weekends with him.

We later established a Friday-to-Friday schedule, alternating weeks at each home, but the girls would come to my house after school each day, regardless of where they were staying that week. During the weeks they spent with Pierre, he picked them up after work. Pierre became bothered by the idea I was able to be with the girls *every* day, when he could be with them only after work every other week. I understood his frustration, even jealousy, and we talked about it on a number of occasions. At one point he suggested getting a babysitter for the after-school times during his week. I explained why it was a true gift that we *all* had me at home and how critical it was for the girls to be with their mother as opposed to a babysitter. He agreed and we continued the pattern.

Pierre always paid child support, but this was still a tough period financially and emotionally. I took on extra jobs and was even on food stamps for a while. At times I did feel sorry for myself, but I soldiered on. I was elated when I landed a teaching job at my children's elementary school as a special-needs para-educator, which relieved some of the financial pressure.

Big Key Point: *We maintain a "we're all in this together" philosophy. As parents, we are forevermore linked to one another and must work for the common good of the family. I try to be gracious and flexible, to go with the flow. If it wasn't Pierre's week with the children but he'd wanted to grab a child and head out on a hike, I supported it joyfully.*

MOVING ON

During the year of separation, I met Jesse. I first laid eyes on him when I began working at an athletic club in Maryland. He was a fitness trainer, and I was working at the front desk handing out keys and towels (think: Tina Fey's account of her stint at the YWCA in her book *Bossypants*). He was very good looking but also very young. He was 21 and I was 33. Still, when he showed an interest, I agreed to go out on a few group dates. I got to know more about him and liked what I saw. We branched out to going on solo dates and our romance just blossomed.

Jesse entered my life when Pierre and I were humming along in our co-parenting. Pierre's initial concern, of course, was, "Who is this guy who will be part of our girls' lives?" Important question! This is when trust, understanding, and time are needed. I knew the three of us had to work together, so the tone of the relationship was important. I can honestly say that I always stayed in the adult and spoke of Pierre only in positive terms. I acted like a matchmaker, I suppose, helping Jesse and Pierre to be their best selves. I was always upbeat when they'd meet, such as during sports games or when Pierre picked up the girls. When the three of us didn't see eye-to-eye on an issue, I would filter the disagreement to Pierre in a gentle way. But Pierre and Jesse also worked very hard to maintain a good working relationship, sprinkling it with laughs and interesting conversations that had nothing to do with the girls.

Jesse was first introduced to the girls as my friend and began spending time with us for hiking, camping, and similar activities. Eventually, I explained that Mr. Cannone, as they used to call him, and I were going to get married. We chose to have a commitment ceremony that included the girls and a party with family and friends, including Pierre and his girlfriend. I commended Pierre for attending, and I thanked Jesse for supporting my need to invite him.

After the wedding, we settled into our new blended family routine. We lived a block from Pierre, so there could be important back and forth time spent with both parents.

For a while, Pierre dated a woman who told him that I wasn't to step foot into his house—my former home where he still lived. Pierre stood firm in his commitment to a healthy, respectful, co-parenting relationship. He told her, "Yes she will! She's the mother of my children and she's *always* welcome." Now, Pierre is married to a lovely woman who has brought warmth and more family members into the girls' lives. She's been a kind "bonus parent" for the girls and that is indeed a gift. But all of this takes trust and time.

Big Key Point: *I am respectful of my former spouse's new relationships and confident that that he will continue to respect me and mine.*

The decision to have children with Jesse was an easy one. I had always wanted a large family, and Jesse agreed. He and I had eight children, five of whom lived, in eight years. Throughout, we continued to work very hard to co-parent with Pierre for our "big girls." Choices we made throughout reflect our views of family and inclusion.

What's in a name, you ask? Nothing and everything! I've chosen to retain the last name from my first marriage. I felt strongly that I wanted to maintain a name-connection with my older daughters. When Jesse and I decided to add to the family, I asked him if the hyphenated name, Verroye-Cannone, could be used for our future children. I also asked Pierre if he would mind us using his last name for my children with Jesse. It took time, discussion, and careful consideration, but eventually, and maybe unbelievably, both men said, "Yes, go ahead."

I do not use the terminology "step-parent" or "step-siblings." I just don't like it. Again, you could argue, what's in a name? But I believe words matters. To me *step* conjures up distance, as in "one step away." "Bonus parent," on the other hand, reminds me of a gift. For the "youngers," as we refer to the five youngest children, when they've asked for details about the "big girls," I'd say simply, "Juliette, Chloe, and Natasha are your sisters." All of the "big girls" call Jesse "Dadjess," so the big girls weren't calling him by his first name, which I think is a mistake, and the "Dad" part was added for the youngers to hear. The youngers refer to Pierre as "Uncle Pierre."

As for "looky-loos" who ask, "Are those all your children?" or "Is this all the same family?" I never break it down to "those are my children with Pierre and those are my children with Jesse." It's all one family. I'm not pretending that there wasn't a divorce or that the DNA of the children isn't different, but this is *our family*.

Big Key Point: *We tried to think creatively about names and titles. There are no hard and fast rules about this, so our family could decide what fits us.*

TALKING IT OUT

Communication is key! I realize that phrase is overused, but it is true nonetheless, especially when you are co-parenting. This can be challenging, though, because marriages often end precisely *because* of poor communication. Have hope! It's never too late to begin talking with each other, and it's vital in keeping the children on the right course. Communicate via paper, email, phone, or in-person away from the children. If a conflict seems unmanageable, by all means seek professional help.

Pierre and I didn't have many parental crises; however, two stand out. One was when Natasha, who was 16 at the time, went walking in the woods with a boy and was not home at dark. I frantically called both Jesse and Pierre, and we worked together to figure out where she was. It turned out that she was fine, but we were upset with her lack of good judgment, and we supported one another in disciplining her.

The other time was when Juliette, then 17, had a party in our basement, without our knowing it, while the rest of the family was on a trip to Florida. I caught wind of the festivities from my girlfriend who had heard Juliette's name mentioned in connection with a known troublemaker. I looked at pictures on Facebook and, lo and behold, the party was at our house. I called Pierre, who went over and read her the riot act, explaining that she could have, through her careless actions, had Dadjess and me thrown in jail, among many other frightening scenarios that could have arisen. Pierre, Jesse, and I then discussed disciplinary measures. For starters, we called my parents, who moved into our house and babysat her for two weeks until our return. I made one or two phone calls to her from Florida, but mostly left her to stew in her own juices. But it felt great for the co-parents to be working from the same sheet of music once again.

Big Key Point: *We refrain from finger-pointing and focus on what really matters, which is raising kind, responsible children. This means sharing and supporting one another in our disciplinary practices.*

Sometimes what's best for the child stinks for the parent! Remember when I talked about Pierre feeling cheated because I got to spend more time with the children because I was a stay-at-home parent? Well, by the time Chloe was a senior in high school, she was the oldest child living at home and was leading a very busy life with school, an internship, sports, and social life. She asked us if she could stay full-time at Pierre's house because she was tired of schlepping her belongings from house to house; plus, she would be nearer to her internship, which was at Pierre's company. Who could blame her? The schlepping is a tiresome drill, and she'd been doing it since kindergarten. I have to be honest: I felt sad that she "chose" Pierre over me/us. I had to work through my feelings and then toss my ego aside to trust that she would want to come hang out. And guess what? She did!

Trust me, when you are divorcing and in the throes of working out co-parenting arrangements, emotions can and do run high. It's easy to feel jealous, left out, and in competition for your children's affection and resort to such tactics as gift-giving and permissiveness. Giving into these feelings will *always* blow up in your face. Find another outlet. When I have issues, I often turn to my posse of girlfriends. I explain to them what's happening, and they help me to sort through my feelings. In the case of Chloe, I came to realize that her decision to stay at Pierre's home and just visit with us was created by her needs. I could've gone to court and argued that it was my right to have her 50 percent of the time. Blah, blah, blah. Instead, I understood that it was important for Chloe to stay put in one house for a change. We all respected her decision.

Big Key Point: *By taking ego out of the equation, we can be mindful about how emotions either help or hinder any given situation. It's not about us. It's about our child/children.*

FINDING BEAUTIFUL

Some folks may read this and think I'm making this stuff up. I hear that "it's too good to be true." Or, "You're lucky that you had a great situation." The truth of the matter is that we all made the choice to behave in a civilized, kind, and compassionate way, and thus created and designed a great situation. We committed to continue walking that path, even when it wasn't easy.

I admit that I am a glass-half-full kind of person. I have learned through experience to trust in another's best intentions. Truthfully, there may be countless examples of frustrations and hardships that occurred over the last nearly two decades, but I choose to focus on the good, the successes, and the triumphs.

Even as I was thinking about this chapter I asked Pierre if I should use a pen name for him, to which he answered, "Sure! 'Mr. Fantastic' works!" I consider myself extremely fortunate to have two wonderful and devoted men with whom to co-parent. Reflecting on this whole story brought me to a greater appreciation for the skills, attitudes, and dedication that Jesse brought to our family. He stepped in and stepped up, joining Pierre and me as co-parents. Jesse recently received a vote of confidence from our daughter Juliette, who sometimes would butt heads with Jesse during her teen years. When she reached the age he had been when he became the head of our complex and growing household, she told us, she realized the commitment he had made, and her understanding of and respect for Jesse grew accordingly.

My mother often shared the story Emily Perl Kingsley, a writer for *Sesame Street,* used as a metaphor to describe the experience of raising a disabled child. She told about a family who planned a dream vacation to Italy. They bought guidebooks and made wonderful, detailed plans to visit all the sites of Italy—Michelangelo's David, the Coliseum, and the gondolas of Venice. They even studied Italian. Finally the day arrived. When their plane landed, the flight attendant announced, "Welcome to Holland!"

"Holland? What? We are supposed to be in Italy!"

"Well," the flight attendant said, "we haven't taken you somewhere that is horrible, disgusting, or filthy; it's just a different place. Now you just have to buy new guidebooks and learn another language."

They looked around and began to notice that Holland was indeed beautiful and enjoyable. Instead of gondolas, they found windmills; instead of Michelangelo, they found Rembrandt.

And so it was for us. We changed course, but we stayed in the boat together, and it brought us safely ashore at a lovely destination.

Recently, Pierre and I had a really meaningful conversation, one that was 17 years in the making. Yep, 17 years! Something profound happened to one of our daughters that necessitated back and forth phone calls between Pierre and me. During one of the calls, we began discussing our marriage and divorce. It was truly the first time we had spoken like that. We each said what our accountability had been and apologized for our shortcomings. Talk about cathartic! I was crying and seriously could not stop. It was so helpful to talk about our marriage and divorce and to commend one another for a job well done in raising our girls.

In the age of quick solutions and one-hour wrap-ups of television plots, we have to keep in mind that problems/feelings/beliefs take time to be understood/sorted through/honored. Just like the story of the family who set out for Italy and landed in Holland, our family's course changed in ways we could never have predicted. It is different than we planned, but I realize that it is indeed beautiful.

I once told a group of high school classmates that my dad had elephant man's disease to encourage kindness and non-judgmental attitudes and that my mom was an Olympic javelin thrower, just to be silly. But I digress. I am the mother of eight children ages 25, 23, 19, 12, 11, 9, 7 and 4. Prior to becoming a mom, I attended Juniata College, obtaining a B.S. in Elementary Education. I used the degree once when I was a special-needs teacher. I currently live on a ranch in Texas with my husband, children, and a whole lot of goats, chickens, bunnies, and ducks.

WILL NO ONE HELP ME?

Advocating for my ADHD child in a system that doesn't understand

Susan Kruger

There is a scene in the Disney movie *Beauty and the Beast* in which Belle is being held prisoner by the Beast. Her father, desperate to rescue her, returns to town, begging for help. The townspeople lead him on, letting him think they will assist him. But, in truth, they think he's a "crazy lunatic." They throw him out the door, where he lands face first in a pile of snow. Lying in the bitter cold, he wails in hopeless desperation, "Will no one help me?"

That scene could almost describe 18 months of my life. My son was a "prisoner" to attention deficit hyperactivity disorder. When I sought support, people thought I was exaggerating the struggles we faced. Or they assumed I was a bad parent.

At age 7, Mark had classic—and highly frustrating—symptoms of ADHD. He was always on the move, distracted, and rarely engaged at school. He couldn't process verbal instructions if his life depended on it. These challenges made parenting incredibly difficult. But the worst, by far, were the mood swings! When he was a kindergartner, they became a regular part of his life—as well as the lives of my husband, daughter, and me. There was no telling when they would hit. Any little thing could trigger a two-hour battle.

These struggles wreaked havoc on our family. It was impossible to get to school—or anywhere—on time. Many evenings and vacations were destroyed by Mark's outbursts. And forget about homework! His reading teachers refused to work with me or extend any compassion. They thought I was a lazy parent when I returned assignments with notes attached saying: "Mark had a massive meltdown last night. I couldn't get him to do his homework. I'm still trying to get medical help, but I'm on a three-month waiting list."

This is a humiliating situation for any parent, but it held an extra sting for me. I am an educator with a national platform. I consult with textbook companies and write for parenting magazines. I am an expert in learning. Specifically, I teach students study skills and help parents manage homework. Still, I was helpless in managing these circumstances.

I *knew* I was dealing with a medical problem, but his teachers thought I was a total sham. The situation was made worse by the fact that Mark was a calm, quiet child in school. The "Mark" that his teachers and principal saw was very different from the "Mark" that would explode at home. I can't blame them for being perplexed. To them, he seemed like an angel. Mark is an angel! He's a lovely soul who loves to please people.

However, two things became obvious to me and my husband. First, Mark's behavior was *not* a ploy to manipulate us or get attention. That did not fit his personality. Plus, many of his meltdowns occurred during activities he *wanted* to do. Why would he sabotage his own fun time on purpose? Second, he was clearly experiencing some sort of chemical imbalance. It was as if he were possessed. On the flip of a coin, his eyes could go blank, and he would lose all capacity to be rational. He could not control himself.

One day, when Mark was in the middle of first grade, we took an hour-and-a-half road trip to visit his favorite people: Uncle Greg, Aunt Mandy, and Katie, who was just two weeks old at the time. Mark was over the moon about being her big cousin. But those 90 minutes dragged into the longest of my life. Mark turned into a sobbing, inconsolable mess. He repeatedly wailed, "I wish I was never even born!" Then, for a brief, five-minute window, he laughed heartily over a crane on the side of the road. The sudden shift was manic and very disconcerting.

By then, I had been trying for months to get help. I was sent from doctor to doctor, waiting list to waiting list. My concerns were dismissed. Just like Belle's father, people thought I was a crazy lunatic. No one said this to my face, but their lack of support and repeated suggestions to improve my parenting skills told me how they really felt.

Around this time, I also began to suspect that Mark had dyslexia. I had noticed several warning signs when I listened to him read. I'm a certified reading specialist and kept notes on my observations. Finally, I gave Mark a formal evaluation. The results confirmed my suspicions.

Just as I was about to call Mark's principal to discuss my concerns, he called us. I was pleased, figuring he had similar concerns about Mark's reading. So, I gathered my notes and the results of the reading assessment to prepare for the conference.

But I was thrown a sucker punch! The principal *was* worried that Mark's reading scores had not improved in the previous six months, since Mark started first grade What I did not expect, however, was to be blamed for the problem.

The principal was troubled that Mark had missed a lot of school. He knew about our medical concerns and all of the doctor appointments; however, he had not seen any sign of distress in Mark at school. He told me, "Since the outbursts are happening only at home, this is a parenting problem." He reached across the table, wagged his finger in my face, and scolded me: "YOU are holding your son back. His MOTHER is holding him back!" He concluded the meeting with a serious threat; if Mark had one more absence, he would report us for "educational neglect," which is child abuse in the court system.

Just like Belle's father, I was thrown out in the cold.

I felt duped! I thought he was our "educational partner." Instead, my integrity as a professional, and more important, as a parent, was challenged. It was an extraordinarily painful accusation. It was also a bully move, abusing his position of authority.

I'm not sure what a panic attack is, but I think I had one that night. I felt physical pain. I had been *killing* myself over Mark. I was worrying myself sick and getting no sleep. I worked late at night because my daytime hours were filled with doctor appointments, medical tests, and childcare during his frequent "sick days." I was falling apart on my child's behalf, only to be insulted and kicked to the curb.

We immediately pulled Mark from that school. I was certain I could bury the principal—and the court—under tons of paperwork, but we couldn't risk a potential fight to keep our child. It was a major setback, but we forged ahead.

We finally found a clinic specializing in formal evaluations for learning challenges. By this time, however, we had learned not to tell doctors or educators about the mood swings. As soon as we did, the attention turned toward us and the quality of our parenting.

My husband and I aren't perfect parents by any means, but we are as prepared as any parents can possibly be! My husband is also a teacher. We have each spent years honing our behavior-management skills in the classroom. We've even had extensive training in "Love and Logic." But I'm here to tell you: *logic* does not prevail in a child with special needs!

The clinical testing took two months, but finally confirmed ADHD and dyslexia. The team of doctors congratulated me on catching the symptoms so early, especially the dyslexia. "Most parents and teachers don't catch this until the child is much, much older," they explained. I burst into tears. I had been vindicated!

THE PATH TOWARD HEALING

When we finally got the green light to begin treatment, we had already spent months trying various diets, ruling out food allergies and anything else suspected as a potential cause of ADHD. Now we pinned our hopes on medication.

My husband and I set clear boundaries about the use of drugs. We agreed that they would be tolerated *only* if they allowed Mark to be his true self. We would not accept personality changes or other negative side effects. We also agreed that Mark would have input; if he didn't feel "right" on a certain medication or dosage, he had veto power. He actually exercised that veto power once, so we moved on to the next option.

It took several months to find the right treatment, but when we did, angels hovered over our house and sang a glorious chorus! We noticed stark improvements overnight. The outbursts were immediately and dramatically reduced. Mark was then capable of working with a counselor; within eight weeks, the mood swings were gone altogether.

We had our Mark back! He still struggled with dyslexia, but he was excelling in his new school. He even became more cooperative over making healthy food choices and joined in sports and other physical activities with confidence.

I've since learned that the mood swings were caused by serious anxiety. Anxiety, it turns out, is a "kissing cousin" to ADHD; the biology of the two disorders are nearly identical. The reason

Mark was *not* having outbursts at school was because he was riddled with fear. At home, without fear to "cork" it, the cycle of anxiety spun through his brain like thread in a sewing machine on full throttle.

There were two factors fueling the distress. First, he was on sensory overload. In his previous school, there were too many people and too much noise and commotion for him to cope effectively. Second, as I was to discover, he had been treated poorly by two teachers and the principal who were impatient with his lack of attention and were excessively mean. I even witnessed one very concerning incident while volunteering in Mark's class one day. It was just a couple of days prior to my meeting with the principal; the pieces of the puzzle snapped into focus very quickly.

It has now been 16 months since Mark's treatment took hold, and I'm happy to report that he is thriving. He enjoys his life and handles emotions in an age-appropriate manner. There have been no more tantrums or evidence of the chemical changes that seemed to overtake him. Thankfully, the other frustrating symptoms of ADHD have also been minimized, allowing me to give him proper support for his dyslexia. He's now in the middle of third grade and a fluent reader!

WHAT DO OTHER PARENTS DO?

I could not be happier about Mark's progress, but one question has haunted me since we encountered our first roadblock: If this is happening to *us,* what is it like for other parents?

We had every resource at our disposal. We are both professional educators. My husband was a highly respected, nationally board-certified teacher in the same district as our son's school. (He even won a prestigious teaching award just 48 hours after the principal's accusations.) My mother is a physician who consistently supported our concerns. She encouraged us to keep fighting and assured us that we weren't crazy. With her support and benefits from my husband's job, we had unlimited access to healthcare. In theory, we had everything we needed to push forward. Yet we were met with unimaginable obstructions.

Over and over again, I would say to my husband, "I am using every ounce of my professional energy to help Mark. Every step of the way, I've had a 'plan B.' If something doesn't work, I'm on to the next thing. I don't know when we'll find an answer, but I know how to keep fighting. What do parents do who don't have our training or our resources?" I still shudder to think about it.

Throughout the ordeal, I had this great sense that I was supposed to be learning from it. It was as though I had two personalities: one was the anxious, sleepless mother; the other was the quiet observer, soaking up every morsel of information and enduring the gamut of emotions. I just knew that God was testing me. I had a very strong sense that it was all happening for a good reason.

I've already seen our trials bring positive outcomes to others. At least a dozen close friends and family members have directly benefited from lessons we learned. It is not unusual for me to log into Facebook and find a message from a friend, asking for information to help her ADHD child. It's becoming a regular occurrence, just within my personal network.

In December 2012, *ADDitude* magazine, a publication dedicated to ADHD, invited me to sit on an expert panel and host a Web chat about school-related ADHD issues. More than 200 questions came in so fast and furious that I couldn't possibly read them all during the one-hour chat. I finally read through all of them the following weekend, while on a road trip with my family.

After getting through only a few dozen questions, I was in anguish for these parents. I vented to my husband, "These questions are just heart-breaking. There is so much pain here! So many people don't understand ADHD and are fighting the stigma.

Children are accused of being lazy. Parents aren't able to get help and think they are crazy. This is just awful!"

Mark suddenly piped in from the backseat, "Yeah, but Mom, you did such a good job of getting me through all of this terrible stuff; you can help them, too."

Wow! There is nothing like an endorsement from your child, especially after walking through the storms we've shared together. He knew this had been my goal all along, but I sure do love how he tries to cheer his mama up.

MAKING A DIFFERENCE

A week after the principal's accusations, I shared the story with the subscribers of my newsletter. It wasn't easy. I knew I didn't do anything wrong, yet I still felt shamed. We had many friends and connections at the school. But after that serious accusation, we evaporated from the community. We didn't talk to anyone. There were no goodbyes; we just disappeared. Who would believe us? I don't even believe it happened.

My subscribers responded with overwhelming support! "If this could happen to you," many wrote back, "I don't feel so bad about what happened to me." Apparently, there are other bullies lurking around, posing as "respected" teachers and administrators. The vast majority of educators are dedicated and compassionate people, so the bullies catch us all off guard.

I had always figured ADHD was about "attention and distraction." I had no idea ADHD could cause so much pain. After doing months of research, I discovered that the disorder is NOT about distraction. It's a power outage on the brain circuits. Specifically, the front cortex of the brain is short on chemicals needed to send strong, consistent neuron signals to the rest of the brain. Instead, many signals are weak and never connect. Imagine cutting a wire between two bulbs on a string of holiday lights; the circuit would be severed and the power would go out. This is exactly what happens in an ADHD brain. It is these short-circuits that cause all sorts of problems.

Through my research to help Mark, I learned that I, too, have ADHD. I finally understand why my kids have to ask me three times to get them something to drink, and why I spin around in circles in the kitchen, taking two hours to cook a "30-minute meal." I have always had a hard time falling asleep, and have experienced chronic fatigue throughout my entire life. My loving husband says that it is often challenging to connect with me. However, I am a very organized person, so I fly under the radar. It turns out that organization is a healthy coping mechanism; one that helps to compensate for my absent-mindedness.

As soon as I began telling others that I have ADHD, people have come out of the woodwork to tell me how ADHD has impacted their lives. Many tell about needing illegal drugs to manage, not to get "high," but simply to focus. Others tell about how the disorder has brought them to or near to divorce. Some have shared stories of how they seem to consistently work against themselves and are extremely frustrated. I lost a beloved cousin at age 56 due to a self-induced accident. In retrospect, I'm absolutely sure she had an undiagnosed case of ADHD.

The condition looks different in every individual based on a variety of factors: varying amounts of brain chemicals, DNA, life experiences, and individual ways of dealing with challenges. Some people develop effective coping strategies; others fall into destructive behaviors. The common thread, however, is a general feeling of not being able to meet one's own potential.

ADHD is a neurological condition that has been around for centuries. Many geniuses throughout the ages had ADHD. But far more people have suffered from addiction or were imprisoned; some are simply shunned for behavior that was always thought to be within their control.

When it is understood and channeled correctly, ADHD provides many blessings: It usually fosters great creativity and intelligence. It amplifies personalities, and it lends itself to deep intuition and compassion for others.

I share our journey in the hopes that it will help those who may be:

- A parent who needs support with an ADHD child.
- An adult who has faced a lifelong battle with this "hidden" condition.
- A friend or teacher to someone who may have ADHD.
- An inspired advocate for someone who has no one else to go to for help.

Susan Kruger, M.Ed., is author of the worldwide, best-selling study skills book, *SOAR® Study Skills*. Susan struggled in K-12, but earned a 3.9 GPA in college after learning study skills. Seventeen years later, as her son struggled with ADHD and dyslexia, she learned she had the same conditions. She spent months researching ADHD, anxiety, and the brain, desperately seeking answers. As a result, she developed The ADHD Circuit,™ a simple model for understanding the biology of ADHD. This model empowers children and adults with ADHD to have a clear understanding of their challenges and build effective detours around them. Learn more at StudySkills.com/adhd.

LIFE ALONG THE BORDERLINE

Confronting my daughter's mental illness

Kay Raypholtz

When I held my daughter in my arms for the first time, I also cradled many hopes and dreams. I looked into that sweet face and saw only good things in her future.

But the months before Tara's birth were emotionally troubled. I became pregnant after dating her father for only six weeks. I was a 21-year-old college student; he was a two-time divorcé with an eight-year-old. His first words upon learning of my condition were that he would pay for the abortion. I refused, and he seemed to accept the fact that he was going to be a parent again.

I moved in with him, but he soon began to pull away from me. Some days, he seemed happy about impending fatherhood; other days he repeatedly played the song "Cinderella" by Firefall, which includes the lyrics: "Cinderella can't you see / Don't want your company / You better leave this mornin' leave today / Take your love and your child away." My heart would break, but I wanted to be a family so badly that I overlooked his cruelty. One day, I could no longer ignore it: He brought one of his ex-wives into our home and introduced her as "the woman I love."

I was mere days from my due date.

My brother came and helped me to make the six-hour trek back home to live with my parents. When Tara was born a few days later, I felt it was a beginning for both of us. Single parenthood was difficult, but being a mommy healed my pain. Tara was my delight.

Then came another devastating blow. My mother had contracted a staph infection three years earlier, and it had slowed her considerably. I knew she wasn't well, but I was blindsided when, at 53, she suffered a heart attack. I believe she was dead before she hit the ground.

I felt totally alone. My champion, the person who loved me unconditionally was gone. I functioned in a daze, and I'm not sure how I managed to care for my own child. But I also had two younger brothers, one still in high school; he needed motherly nurturing too. Our father was grieving in his own way, drowning his sorrow at a bar every evening.

In the years that followed, I often wondered whether the traumatic events had an impact on my daughter. Did my turmoil when I was pregnant affect her? Did I fail to nurture her properly when I was grieving the loss of my mother?

UNCONTROLLABLE RAGE

Nothing seemed amiss until Tara was nine months old. She was playing on the floor one night and began to scream and cry. She rolled violently across the room and slammed herself against the bottom of the couch. She was inconsolable. I was ready to take her to the emergency room when she calmed down as suddenly as she had begun the outburst. She quietly fell asleep.

The next morning, I noticed her first tooth breaking through her gums. Did this explain her behavior? As I reflected on what I witnessed the night before, I felt that she had been reacting more in anger than in pain, as though she were angry for feeling pain. It had not seemed "normal."

There was no doubt that my child had a temper, but her tantrums didn't seem to be regular tantrums. She would throw herself to the floor or against furniture, raging at the top of her lungs. If windows were open when she threw a fit, neighbor kids would run to see what the ruckus was all about.

I sought help from the family doctor. He said to ignore the tantrums and go into another room. That didn't help at all. Even though I didn't seek advice from anyone else, I sure received a lot of it. I was told to spank her, sit her in a corner, make her take naps, be firmer, be easier on her, feed her differently, pray over her. People clearly blamed me for the way she acted.

Tara was incredibly stubborn. If she didn't want to do something, she would NOT do it. One seasoned parent tried to show me how to take charge when Tara didn't want to pick up toys she'd been playing with. He was after her for almost an hour, but Tara wouldn't give in. I have to admit that I listened with more than a little self-satisfaction. At least one couple would now believe that I was truly having difficulties.

When Tara was five years old, I took her to a therapist. He said she might be exhibiting signs of oppositional defiant disorder, but then she played happily during our sessions there. Where was the rage she was showing me? After a few weeks, the therapist told me that he had children in his office with problems, but Tara wasn't one of them. I felt my hope seep away.

Tara had moments when she was a little pistol, but she was also sweet and loving and had a great sense of humor. Since it had been just her and me alone for over six years, we had a tight bond. I think that is what helped us through the tough times. There were plenty to come.

When Tara was six, I married a divorced man with two sons. We had a short courtship and tried to get pregnant right away. But less than a year into the marriage, when I was two months pregnant, he left me; we were separated for a year. We reunited after the birth of our son, and Tara seemed thrilled to have a daddy. Four years later, another son was born.

REBELLION AND SELF-DESTRUCTIVE ACTS

When Tara was 12, there were more signs of rebellion. I was working second shift at a local factory, and I was called home one evening because she had disappeared. It was long past bedtime, and we didn't know where she was. I was about to call the police when she showed up.

When she was 14, she twice stayed away overnight. The first time, the police even brought in tracking dogs. Both times, she returned of her own accord the next day, seemingly unconcerned about the fear she'd caused. I put her into diversion counseling at the juvenile probation department after the first incident; the next time, she was charged as an unruly child and spent six months on probation.

Another night I received a frantic phone call at work from my husband. Tara had overdosed on over-the-counter pills. When I arrived at the hospital, her stomach had been pumped. I felt relief, followed quickly by anger. Should I hug her or hit her? There she was, recently so despondent as to attempt suicide, yet she was laughing and talking to the doctors and nurses. I didn't know what to think. An ambulance took her 60 miles away to a mental health facility for youth. She was held in the pediatric intensive care unit overnight. I sat with her as she slept peacefully. Around us were tiny babies in incubators, clinging to life. The irony was even more heart breaking.

The next morning, a psychiatrist, who saw her outside of my presence, said she could be released, as she didn't appear to be depressed. I was aghast, although I would later realize how very good she was at fooling professionals.

Fortunately, a nurse advised me to request a second consult where I could give my input. Tara was seen by a different psychiatrist, and the decision was made to place her in their mental-health facility. She spent nine days there—until the insurance company said it was time to go. She was sent home with instructions to contact a local counselor for further treatment. It took us a week to get an initial interview, after which we had to wait a couple months for an appointment.

Two weeks after she returned home, she swallowed a bottle of Tylenol. Back to the hospital. After another short stay, she was released with instructions simply to see a therapist. We were still weeks away from our previously scheduled appointment. In desperation, I called the mental-health facility where she had stayed, but they would not re-admit her.

Tara had been prescribed antidepressants, but she was not taking them. There was no way to force compliance. Somehow we made it through the summer, and she began therapy with a counselor we both liked. That fall, Tara entered high school as a freshman.

FAILURE OF SUPPORT SYSTEM

I was working third shift and was sleep deprived most of the time. It was difficult to sleep during the day with two active little boys. One day, my two-year-old got croup; it was so severe it required a run to the emergency room. I had two hours of sleep over two days before I was finally able to drift off to sleep.

An hour later, I heard pounding on the door. It was the school superintendent with Tara. I was still in a daze from being awakened when I was told that she had again overdosed on over-the-counter pills. At the hospital, I must have looked a mess from the lack of sleep. The nurse kept asking if I was okay. She even offered me a bed! I noticed Tara getting angry about the attention I was receiving.

When a mental-health professional finally spoke with her, the only advice we received was to continue her counseling—and that she would like to go horseback riding! Excuse me? The answer to my daughter's problem was to go horseback riding? I exploded, responding that if we weren't paying for all Tara's damn hospital bills and therapy appointments, there would be more money for fun stuff! I think Tara was just blowing smoke, because she'd never expressed this desire to me. Again, I saw how she could play the professionals.

The doctor came into the room, and without even the benefit of a drug screening, released her, saying, "I can tell you're a smart girl. Here's a copy of the *Christian Science Monitor*. Take this home and read it; you'll be fine." I was stunned.

Then I found out that Tara had purchased the Tylenol during her school lunch break. She told two friends she had taken the pills, and they ran to the guidance counselor. Instead of responding immediately, the counselor snapped, "I have a meeting. I can't deal with this now." It was an hour and a half before she attempted to contact me, but I had turned off the phone ringer. By the time Tara arrived with the superintendent, a couple of hours had already elapsed. I was furious!

But the roller-coaster ride wasn't over yet. That evening, Tara decided she wanted to visit friends. When I went to stop her, she pushed past me and ran out. A neighbor boy offered to trail her on his bike. When I told the police of the circumstances, they responded right away. With the help of the neighbor, they quickly found her and took her to the station, where we were told she couldn't be held because she hadn't broken a law. I felt she could be safe only if she were locked up, but I was told I could be charged with neglect if I refused to take her home. I literally was beyond being able to think and sat in tears. I must have seemed like a madwoman.

When I hear someone say, "Why didn't you try to get help for her?" I remember that day. We were failed by all of the people who were supposed to help us. People have asked why I didn't file a formal complaint or lawsuit against the doctor or the guidance counselor. One reason was that my father was mayor of the town and running for re-election. I didn't want to call negative attention to the family. But I also believe that I was then a shadow of the woman I am today. I felt defeated. I was constantly sleep deprived, and I was married to a man who was emotionally abusive. I just didn't have the strength.

Tara's high school years were difficult. She didn't complete assignments and failed many classes. She continued to have the rages. She came home stoned one night, and I had her arrested for drug abuse. I know this sounds harsh, but with Tara lessons had to be dramatic. And it eventually dawned on me that Tara didn't really want to die; she always told someone when she overdosed. She was seeking attention.

Up to this point, her diagnosis remained depression. When she was 16 or 17, she became obsessed with a boy, and when he moved out of state, she took a pin and carved a picture of a snake on her ankle. I reported this to her psychologist, and she sent Tara to a psychiatrist. It was then that we first received the diagnosis "borderline personality disorder." I had never heard of this condition, but when I researched it online, everything clicked. Of the eight criteria for diagnosing the illness, she met seven.

It bothered me that a history of abuse and neglect was often associated with the BPD. I have never been aware of her experiencing such trauma. I began to question if my emotional state during my pregnancy and the death of my mother had been a factor. People had always blamed my parenting for her behavior—I didn't set enough limits, I set too many limits, and on and on and on. Even my closest friends questioned me. No one understood. I once was talking to my father about what was wrong with Tara, and he said, "YOU are what's wrong with Tara." How could even my own father believe I was a horrible parent?

NO LONGER ALONE

I joined an email support group for parents of children with BPD. Many had even worse struggles than mine. The common thread was that we were all good parents who had no trouble with our other children, but were frustrated by a son or daughter with BPD. For the first time, I didn't feel alone.

Part of what helped me in the email group was reading what other parents wrote about their own children and asking for their help when I was having issues with my daughter. They talked about tough love and about not playing into their games. I learned the importance of this when, by chance, I didn't go to the hospital when my daughter attempted suicide for the third time. She didn't get the attention she was used to getting and the behavior stopped for a long time. It was later that I read about this strategy in a book called *Stop Walking on Eggshells.* My instincts had been right. It was very hard to not run to help her, but I knew that if I went to the rescue, she would give me more reasons to come to the rescue, i.e., more suicide attempts. In some ways, I felt a release by not having to go. My attention only seemed to feed into her illness. When she was still at home, I made sure she kept attending her regular counseling sessions. She had a good counselor who really helped. When Tara was no longer living at home, I would provide her transportation to her counselor as often as possible.

In the years since the diagnosis, Tara has continued to struggle. It is difficult for her to hold a job for even a year. She filed for disability but was denied. She has been evicted from apartments after losing jobs and failing to pay rent. She has spent months sleeping on a friend's couch or floor. She has been homeless. For a while, she lived out of a car, and even chose three days in jail at one point rather than go back to that car. She has come to my door after two days of not eating.

She has had several more suicide attempts. I've lost count of how many. Each time it has been pills, and each time she has told someone what she has done. Once she swallowed a bottle of Tylenol, along with sleep aids and muscle relaxants. She tried to find a friend to come over to talk to her and was near passing out when someone finally arrived. People were stunned that I wouldn't go to see her in the hospital. Thankfully, I was working as a counselor in an agency and had a supervisor who understood when I told him that she loved to be rescued and that giving her attention only seemed to make things worse. I learned that there is a type of therapy for those with BPD called dialectical behavioral therapy that follows a similar philosophy. Yes, you get the individual to a hospital to be treated, but he or she is back to work the next day.

I sometimes wonder how I got through it all. I enjoyed mothering my sons, neither of whom have mental-health issues. Another thing that helped was having hobbies. I enjoyed talking with friends and designing Web pages. I took time to read and went out with my husband, although we divorced after Tara finished high school. I had to let Tara direct and live her own life, as I had to go on and live my own.

Tara is now 32 and has been married for three years. They have no children, but she maintains a job. She attends counseling sporadically and is not consistent with taking medication. She still struggles with depression, but to most people, she appears to be a happy, bubbly woman who is fun to be around.

She has made real progress. I was proud when she went through a separation from her husband without attempting suicide. A few months ago, she was feeling unstable but instead of doing anything rash, she asked me to take her to a crisis center. She will never be cured of BPD, but she has learned healthier ways to cope.

I've had to change my expectations for Tara. She didn't graduate from high school, but she completed four years of schooling and a cosmetology course. Later, she earned a GED. She has always found a way to work and paid her own way. I've had to realize that my dreams for her were not the same as her dreams for herself. Sometimes I've had to watch her fail.

My dream for her now is for her to have a long and happy life. But I know that is not under my control, and it is always in the back of my mind that I may outlive my daughter.

But just as I knew the day she was born, I do have a beautiful daughter. Her smile lights up a room. She is smart, and she has survival skills beyond anything I could imagine. She is a true survivor.

We still have a special bond, and I like and admire the person she has become. I love her just the way she is.

Kay (Shatzer) Raypholtz is a nontraditional student at Defiance College in Ohio studying for a bachelor's degree in social work after earning an associate's degree in human services. She is a part-time reporter for a local newspaper, and has been married to Mike, a United Methodist pastor, for two years. She has three grown children and two high-school-aged step-children. In the past, she has worked in a factory, as a chemical dependency counselor, and as a caregiver to a profoundly disabled teen. Kay is a native of Montpelier, Ohio, and lives in nearby Pioneer, Ohio.

FROM SHAME TO FREEDOM

The unexpected gifts of an eating disorder

Laurel Hodory

When I came to, I was lying on my side, looking at my sister's twin bed. From that viewpoint, everything appeared sideways. My head pounded, and there was a bit of drool on the bedding.

I was seven years old, alone in the bedroom I shared with my older sister, playing the passing out game. I would take a bandana, tie it around my neck and pull it tight until I blacked out. It gave me something I desperately wanted: escape.

I was trying to flee a hostile, unsafe home environment. Oh, we had a nice home, a well-used country club membership, expensive ski vacations, and new cars as graduation gifts. But it was all a cover for what was really going on. I remember thinking more than once, "No one would believe this," as I hid behind the couch, watching my parents have a knock-down-drag-out fight. On one occasion, my father broke my mother's arm. Once he beat the living daylights out of my older brother with a tennis racket. I frequently saw my father hit my siblings, but somehow I can't recall it happening to me. I don't know if I've blocked it out or if I just got lucky.

Part of what got me through was having siblings to share in the torment. My sister, Marcie, was three years older, and she always gave me a sense of stability and safety, especially during those nights when Dad would come home drunk, stomping angrily toward our bedroom, and my heart was racing with pending doom. Tim was 18 months older than I. We were like oil and water. He had an immature sense of humor that I found annoying instead of funny. Maybe it was his way of coping with the abuse he endured. He was subjected to, by far, the most assaults. We all protected our younger brother, David. He was a cutie but also the family genius. Although we were all straight-A students, David was a National Merit Scholar and computer whiz kid.

We didn't talk about the troubles between Mom and Dad, the violence, or the reign of terror by our father. We were too afraid. But we shared an unspoken bond and took comfort in one another's presence during episodes of rage. Outside social interactions were carefully chosen and limited. The vast majority of my memories are about being with David, Marcie, and Tim.

Dad, who also grew up in a dysfunctional family, had big ambitions. He fulfilled them when he became a dentist, then an orthodontist, then a real-estate tycoon of sorts. But he was an alcoholic, and when he got drunk, he got angry. He also had a lot of women friends who would sometimes show up at the house at odd hours, drunk and cursing him in the front yard.

My major goal was to hide so I couldn't get hurt. If I couldn't physically hide, I could certainly conceal what I really felt and thought. I learned how to pretend to be the daughter my parents wanted me to be—one who got good grades, did household chores, and went to church, whether I liked it or not.

My mother was a devout Jehovah's Witness, and we children were coerced into attending services five hours each week and following the rigid rules. No holidays, including birthdays, were celebrated. And there were unspoken expectations; for example, as children, we were not to have any needs, feelings, or opinions. It seemed as though our only purpose was to meet the demands of our parents, whose lives were riddled with chaos, drama, and crises driven by alcoholism, infidelity, abuse, and narcissism.

We were taught to put work before play, and there was always more work to be done. On weekends, our father would wake us early and take us to one of his many properties to paint, buff floors, plant flowers, or do whatever maintenance was needed. The worse part was that his demands on our time interfered with plans we made with friends. It was a vicious cycle of control and disappointment that ultimately impacted our social development.

Because my father kept my mother on a shoestring budget, there were times when I was afraid to ask for lunch money for fear it would launch my mother into a guilt-inducing tirade. Occasionally, our phone service or electricity was turned off because our father hadn't provided enough money for Mom to pay the bills. Yet, we had so many luxuries, such as expensive ski vacations and new cars. It was confusing!

When I found myself upset, angry, or hurt, I threw myself into sports, excelling in many areas. I was voted "most valuable" on the swimming, soccer, and basketball teams. I mastered academics too, taking advanced placement classes in hopes that the teachers would see my goodness. I graduated at the top of my class, but still I didn't feel "good."

STUFFING AND HIDING WITH FOOD

Then I found a new escape: food.

When I was 15, my hormones kicked in. The maelstrom of emotions was almost unbearable. That summer, I began hanging out at the country club pool, and that's where my eating disorder was born. My girlfriends and I would lay out in the sun all day, slathered in Bain de Soleil tanning oil. To look good in our Gottex swimsuits, we'd starve ourselves, drinking iced Tab and dining only at the end of the day on shrimp cocktail or something equally light. The fasting was important, too, because at night, there were parties to attend, and we knew the alcohol we'd consume contained a lot of calories.

Then I fell head over heels in love. John was lean with broad shoulders, and a slightly tousled, boy-next-door innocence about him. Things quickly got hot and heavy. But 16 was an awkward stage for me. I felt a mix of sexual yearnings and at the same time a repulsion of them. I also had a fear and mistrust of men stemming from my father's treatment of my mother and his girlfriends. It didn't help that my social skills were weak, and I was ashamed of my looks and boyish figure.

I had been able to hide my alcohol binges from my parents for a summer or two, but then they discovered my secret. I was grounded indefinitely and had to break up with John. I was sad, but in a way, I was also relieved.

Pain and confusion mounted inside me, and somehow I thought the solution was to not eat.

I wanted the freedom to explore myself as a young adult. Yet I always had a harsh curfew, and I wasn't allowed to spend the night at a friend's house, see R-rated movies, or date. I began to openly rebel against my parents' rules.

I would head out with my friends for an evening of partying. Invariably, alcohol would be served. Combined with the fasting, I often unwittingly drank more than I could handle. When I'd arrive home, if I was lucky, my mom would have fallen asleep. But more often then not, she was awake, waiting to test my sobriety and interrogate me on what I'd been doing. After the inquisition, I'd curl up in bed up with a sleeve of saltines that I would quickly demolish. Then another. And another. Then I'd vomit them up secretly, quietly in the bathroom before I fell asleep for the night.

I was obsessed with being thinner. I had big feet and a muscular, athletic build. When I'd moan to my mother, she'd say, "You're not fat. Just big. Maybe if you got really thin, you'd look smaller." I took her message to heart. If I were thin enough, I would finally be able to feel good about myself. *Thin* would make my problems go away. *Thin* would mean that I would finally be accepted, not criticized.

I alternated between fasting and giving in to food but then heaving it up. This cycle of starving yourself, followed by barely eating and then forcing yourself to throw up is called bulimarexia, an eating disorder that intersects the symptoms of both anorexia and bulimia.

At first, I was able to maintain my uber-thinness. But I started to stuff myself and then vomit—daily. I mostly did it at home, after everyone had gone to bed. But I also sometimes did it at school or in the bathhouse at the country club. Binging somehow helped me to feel in control. I was able to hide my true feelings and thoughts, to keep them suppressed. This is where the food came in handy. I could literally shove down the very thing that was trying to bubble up inside me.

My schedule was insane. Twice a week, I played basketball. I'd leave for school at 7 a.m. and get home at 11 p.m., without having had dinner. I'd be exhausted from a grueling game and perhaps facing a large term paper project due in AP English the next day. I'd stay up, working and devouring Kroger's yellow round tortillas or Little Debbie Nutty Buddy bars, whatever I could get my hands on.

The bulimarexia quickly escalated into bulimia. I'd stuff myself anytime I was alone at home, sneaking a little bit of a lot of different foods so that no one would catch me. I got really good at being very, very quiet when I threw up. Sometimes, I would have thrown up so many times that the toilet wouldn't flush anymore.

One time I had to pull the stopper out of the sink and use it instead. I remember once the bathroom smelled bad and there was a plumbing problem. I had no doubt that I was the cause, but of course I kept silent. There were other signs to cover up: My eyes would be bloodshot from the pressure in my face from continuous vomiting; I went through volumes of Visine.

I had always wanted with all my heart to attend the University of Colorado in Boulder, but my parents wouldn't hear of it. They had expectations that we would go to college and the finances to pay for it, but the idea of a child moving out of state was out of question. I searched for a university that offered scholarships based on academic merit, not financial need.

At last, I was accepted on a 50 percent academic scholarship to Washington University in St. Louis, Missouri. I was thrilled! Surprisingly, my parents allowed me to accept and I enrolled for the 1985-86 academic year.

But when I got there, I found that the years of restrictive parenting had dampened my spirit. I felt painfully ill at ease in social circles. My dis-ease led me to hide behind my food addiction. I stole food from my roommates, and visits to the "porcelain goddess" became even more frequent. The binging and purging could go on by the hour. When I was too sick and exhausted to continue, I'd pass out. When I awoke, I had an immense sense of self-disgust, yet somehow I felt lighter.

I saw myself as a glutton. I was out of control. I had no will power. I hated myself. What made matters worse, because of my height, swings of 10 to 15 pounds easily went unnoticed. Others couldn't tell that I was battling such a destructive behavior. The shame I felt about my inability to control my eating disorder masked other shames—those I felt about my womanhood, my creativity, my independence.

BOTTOMING OUT BRINGS EPIPHANY

During my sophomore year, I secretly planned for months to attend spring quarter in Paris. I was a French major/Art History minor, and I knew I would never become fluent without travel. Plus, I had a deep desire to explore, fed by childhood ski and sailing vacations and the example of aunts who frequently visited Europe. It felt natural to me to want to study abroad. But somehow this idea was viewed as frivolous by my parents.

I was desperate for something—anything—that was authentically mine. Everything in my life had been decided for me. So I set about masterfully planning to finance the trip without my parents' help. And I did it. I got funding from a part-time job and the support of one of my aunts. I was worried about how my parents would react, but I reasoned I was safe because I no longer lived at home.

Then the worst thing happened: The program was cancelled. My devastation drove me to three days of gluttony. It was horrible.

But on the third day, in the midst of my feeding frenzy, I had a moment of pure, still, focused clarity: I was not gorging myself because I lacked self-control; I was trying to shove down my disappointment.

It was like God had written it on a neon sign.

The realization was utterly shocking but, at the same time, a relief. I knew in that moment that I had an eating disorder, and I understood why! I picked up the phone and called the student health center.

Within a week, I sat in the office with a counselor, explaining my behavior with food. I half expected her to say, "So what? That's normal." But she didn't. Instead, she said, "I think you have an eating disorder." I felt like I had been diagnosed with a terrible disease, not unlike cancer. I was assigned to group therapy, but after my first session, because I had no idea how to process my grief and sense of overwhelm, I went into a weeklong tailspin.

I slowly realized that I wasn't the only one with this problem. I began to acknowledge the plethora of emotions and desires I had been suppressing for years. Still, I couldn't get a handle on the behavior. I was like an addict.

A DREAM COME TRUE BRINGS INSPIRATION

One day, a friend did a class presentation about a castle in France he had helped to renovate. He told of plans to return the following summer. In an instant, I decided to go too. I could finally fulfill the dream I thought I had lost. And this time, I did it on my own—with no help even from my aunt.

The night before we left, I made a promise to myself: I would never again binge-purge. I got on the Air Egypt flight on July 22, 1987, and flew to freedom. And I've kept that promise ever since. It was as if taking control of my life gave me the power to take control of my eating disorder.

In the ensuing years, I've learned that it is rare for a teen—or for that matter, anyone—to kick an eating disorder. They are among the toughest addictions to heal because the addictive substances cannot be permanently removed. The inspiration, strategies, and support that helped me out of my illness were many. The Wilce Health Center at The Ohio State University was a godsend. I started out with weekly group therapy and graduated into individual counseling with someone trained in eating disorder recovery.

The work in the early days was startlingly simple, but the tough part was identifying the emotions I was stuffing down. I often found myself intellectualizing and telling a story of why I was upset rather than actually allowing myself to feel the hurt, anger, frustration, disappointment, or grief. I remember being completely clueless as to how to identify particular mental states. The counselor had to give me a chart featuring faces expressing different emotions. I spent several years dredging up and identifying buried emotions. It was work!

My recovery began when I promised not to purge again. But that led me into another disorder: compulsive overeating. I had to devise a plan wherein anytime I had the compulsion to eat, I would wait 20 minutes. If I still wanted to eat after that, I could. But during those 20 minutes, I would read something inspiring. I read every book by Geneen Roth. I also wrote in my journal, a life-saving strategy I had been using since the fourth grade. It was the only place where I felt safe to express my darkest fears and deepest secrets.

Another great support was my athletics. Although I never spoke to any of my teammates about my eating disorder, just being part of team was powerful, almost like family. Because my team members valued me, a void was filled. My ability to perform various physical activities gave me the strength and confidence that carried me through difficult years.

I also used 12-step programs and attended meetings for Adult Children of Alcoholics. Through them, I learned how my own co-dependency was blocking my light. At those meetings, talk about God was difficult for me to accept because of my past with the Jehovah's Witnesses, which involved having religion shoved down my throat. I focused intensely and listened to the wise words to "take what you like and leave the rest."

During graduate school, I enrolled in modern dance classes. Through them I was first introduced to yoga in 1992. I was hooked immediately. Yoga was like no other exercise I had ever done. I found myself totally engaged with what was being taught. My mind didn't try to run off to think about what I could or couldn't eat, or any of the things on my to-do list. I dropped into a deep sense of peace and safety that I had never experienced before. My anxiety disappeared. Instead of being fearful of living alone, I signed a lease on a one-bedroom apartment. I was able to retreat into a private sanctuary in which I could heal. It was one of the most powerful choices I have ever made.

For a long time, yoga simply gave me a visceral experience of what it's like to feel grounded, safe, and whole. But as I practiced more, I also started to lose my distaste for the word *God*. I became curious about how God was dwelling within me. Through my body, I began to develop my own form of spirituality and my own relationship with the Divine.

When I left home for college at age 18, I could never have guessed that I'd be making a career of my spiritual path by becoming a yoga teacher. I found great inspiration in the practices and people I met along the way. In a world where we have been coached out of feeling emotions and bodily sensations in the name of logic and intellect, there is a profound wisdom stored within our bodies, there for all to tap into if we are given the tools.

When I graduated with my master's degree in environmental communications, I went to work to save the planet. Five years into it, I realized I could help the planet more if I could show people how to wake up and take care of their first home—their bodies. Once that connection is made, stewardship for the planet is a natural outgrowth. In 2000, I took a leap of faith to fulfill a new dream: I opened the first dedicated yoga center in my town. Since then, I've been teaching yoga and guiding others in recovering their authentic selves using the tools and strategies that transformed me.

Laurel Hodory, MS, E-RYT500, is a seeker of authenticity and wellness. She is the founder of Yoga with Laurel and leads retreats, workshops, corporate wellness, and yoga teacher trainings internationally that teach participants how to crack the code of their innate, embodied wisdom. Yoga has helped Laurel to recover a healthy relationship with food, herself, and others. She believes it can help almost anyone on their journey—including you! Part coach and part teacher, Laurel inspires her clients to live boldly. She and her husband David live in Columbus, Ohio. Visit www.laurelhodory.com

GETTING OFF THE BIPOLAR ROLLER COASTER

Stepping onto solid ground after learning to stop the ride

Nicole Friedler Brisson

I can't say when it started again: when getting out of bed became a struggle, when weekends seemed to loom vast and empty, when the greatest pleasure I had was moving between places and activities, hoping to stay suspended in time. At some point, the sidewalks seemed to tilt downward, and slowly, after it was too late, I realized that I was sinking. Again.

My walks to work through Central Park, usually enjoyable, became a time of anxiety, yet it was the most doable part of my day. I wasn't home; I wasn't at work. My clothes seemed to expand because my body started to shrink. I lost 30 pounds in one month without dieting or changing my exercise routine. I just wanted to disappear. And things got out of control. Again.

I lost all track of time. If you have never been clinically depressed, it might not make sense to you, but in my depressions, each of which lasted an agonizing nine and a half months, time became convoluted and torturous and backward. Five minutes took three hours to happen as I lay in bed in the fetal position, willing myself to get up, feeling the weight of the day like an anvil on my stomach, unable to move. I'd chide myself to take one step at a time, "Get up. Shower." Then I'd roll to the other side and curl up in as small a ball as possible, shivering uncontrollably while sweating through my nightshirt.

This repeated itself day after day after day.

I did everything to help myself get better. I went to all of my psychiatrist appointments—three times a week for years. I took the prescribed medication, but then felt even worse when, after months, there was no relief. I plodded through my daily routines in slowed-down internal agony, hoping that I would get up one morning and feel better. I lost friends. I was stuck.

At the end of each bout of major depression, I would suddenly feel better when the medication started to work. It was as if blackout shades had been lifted from the windows in my brain. I felt joyous and light and happy, almost too happy. I could feel the difference between hot and cold, taste food, see color, and get back into the sense of time that eluded me for so long. Life was wonderful. I was never going to feel that horrible again. Or so I thought.

This is the story of my diagnosis and recovery from what can be a debilitating, life-stealing disease: bipolar disorder.

AND IT STARTED...

I remember having the deep-seated feeling from a very young age that my life was meant to be "good," that I was supposed to be successful, fulfilled and happy. I was a rule-follower. I went to Smith College and was a good student, singing in an a cappella group and concentrating on my love of photography.

I had no idea what hit me when, at 19, I started feeling lousy during my junior year abroad in Paris. My thoughts became obsessive, the negative ones playing in an endless loop. I was my harshest critic, telling myself how stupid, ugly, useless, (fill in the blank) I was. I had no idea what was happening and feared I would never get better. My mother made me swear that, if I had suicidal thoughts, I would immediately tell someone. She convinced me that killing myself would be the most selfish thing I could do; I would be released, but the people who loved me would be shattered. At my lowest, I would hear her voice and figuratively step away from the edge.

I fell in love with photography in 1987 while taking a hiatus from college after Paris, and when I returned to school I took as many photo courses as possible. My dream was to have one of my photographs accepted into the Museum of Modern Art in New York and to get a graduate degree in photography so I could teach and pass on my love of the art. The day before my graduation, as I was showing my father my senior thesis project hanging on the walls of the art building, he said, "You're a great photographer, but you'll never make a living doing it." I packed away my dream and, ironically, moved to New York City and got my first job—in the Photography Department of the Museum of Modern Art.

I worked there for three and a half years before my second major depression forced me out on disability. I was hospitalized for a month because my psychiatrist put me on 10 different medications within 10 weeks, causing a serious "shortage" in my brain that left me suicidal. Upon returning to my job, I knew it was time to leave permanently, and I realized that museum work was not going to be my career. My grandmother, who lived in Mexico, invited me down for a respite and I accepted. I studied Spanish and fell in love with the country. I returned to New York six months later, seemingly rejuvenated.

THE WHIRLING DERVISH

After each depressive episode, my mood would lift precipitously, and I would be on top of the world, like I was when I was in Mexico. I would feel super-energized for two to three months and then I would be stable for a year and a half or so. Nine months in, I would stop taking my medication because I felt great and figured that the worst had passed. And then the bottom would fall out again. This pattern recurred through the remainder of my time in New York. When the clouds lifted, I was again in an excessively happy place. I was meeting new people everywhere—through work, at coffee shops, walking in Central Park, on trips—and making "friends." I had all kinds of grand ideas for a new career. Once, after meeting Jodie Foster's personal assistant at a dinner in L.A., I wrote Jodie a letter suggesting she hire me to help build her photography collection. There were so many things I wanted to do, I didn't want to choose just one. Once, when trying to figure out what to do with my life while in between jobs, I made business cards for my new "consulting" company—consulting on what, I don't know, I called it Whirling Dervish. Looking back, I realize how out of control I was and how stereotypical my behavior was of the illness.

At 27, during my third serious struggle with depression, nothing was helping me out of the black hole. I had stopped taking my medication after my last bout ended, and when I went back on it, it didn't work. I found another psychiatrist, my fourth or fifth in the course of my illness, who explained that I wasn't just depressed; I was suffering from bipolar depression. One of the clues for him was a hallmark of bipolar patients: they stop taking their medication when their moods lift because they think they're okay or because the hypomanic or manic episodes feel so good. He took a new approach to treatment, prescribing twice the highest dose of antidepressant recommended plus a medication for mood stabilization. Initially, I resisted taking medication that would "brand" me as bipolar, but when I realized there were no noticeable side effects and I was stable, I stopped resisting.

There is an infinite spectrum of the illness: from my manifestation of being primarily depressed followed by bouts of "happy" to those with full-on mania. My happy times were classic hypomania, characterized by fast speech, inflated self-esteem, expansive ideas, and excessive involvement in pleasurable activities with a high potential for painful consequences, such as unrestrained buying sprees or increased sexual activity. My mania was considered mild. I was not hallucinating or standing on rooftops yelling to Jesus, nor was I violent or dangerous to others or myself, which are the characteristics most people think of when they hear "bipolar." They assume it means undiagnosed, untreated, or noncompliant patients who are severely manic and exhibiting crazy behavior.

GETTING OFF THE RIDE

The term *bipolar* had not yet come into public discourse in 1995, when I was first diagnosed. I searched online for information, but not much was available. Today, the term is tossed about in casual conversation and depicted in movies and TV shows. Several celebrities have told their stories, raising public awareness of the illness. Treatment and medical understanding of the disorder have improved immeasurably since then, and there are new medications mass-marketed everywhere (Abilify, for example) using the term bipolar in their literature. To live a healthy life with bipolar disorder takes compliance with medical treatment, hard work in therapy, and acceptance of the illness.

The first thing I had to come to grips with is that bipolar disorder is a disease, just like diabetes or high blood pressure. I also had to accept the necessity of staying on medication. Forever.

I was prescribed Lamictal, which was approved for the treatment of mood disorders around the time I was diagnosed. I stepped back and took a hard look at the years behind me and what had happened when I went off my medication. Through an objective lens, I could see how painfully deep my depression was and how reckless I had been in my hypomanic phases. Taking control of and changing my life was imperative. Once I was properly medicated, committed to getting better, and able to see my past clearly, I stopped bullshitting my therapist and myself. It was hard work and it was expensive, but it was the most important investment I've ever made.

LIFE CHANGER

I had one more depression to live through, although its severity and length were half of what the others had been, due to being on the proper medication, and it wasn't followed by a hypomanic episode. When I was 31, I realized that I had spent most of my life after college listening to other people talk about what they thought I "should" do. Nothing really fit. Another depression began because I was in yet another dead-end job and I knew New York was not the place for me.

I decided that being fired was the best option because I could collect unemployment. So I took a two-week vacation by just walking out the door. (I spent the whole time in bed.) They didn't fire me, and my depression didn't end. I was unable to go back to work after those two weeks and I had to go out on disability again. The day before I was to return, I was told that, due to a reorganization, my position no longer existed. With that pressure gone, my mood started to improve. I took a breath and tried to figure out my next step.

Many of the decisions I've made that might have seemed

impulsive have proven to be the most important and intelligent of my life. I have learned to trust my intuition. What came next was life-changing. My family was worried that I had flipped into hypomania again because of the speed in which things occurred. In mid-August, while balancing my checkbook, I remembered that I had sent a room deposit to a bed-and-breakfast on Martha's Vineyard for a June wedding I planned to attend, but cancelled when I became depressed. It hadn't been refunded, so I called the owner who apologized and went into a long explanation of how busy the summer had been and how she had lost the help she had for the summer. When she learned I wasn't working, she asked if I would like to come help her. I was flabbergasted yet intrigued. How could I just take off when I was on the tail end of another depression? My mom thought it would be good for me, but my father wasn't so sure. A friend of his said to me, "You have to go!" and I was lucky that she said it right in front of him.

Five days later I arrived on Martha's Vineyard. Over the next six weeks, Eleanor and Dave, the owners, "adopted" me. I worked at the B&B four days a week and at a car rental agency for Dave two days a week. I was making $8 an hour and had never been happier. My job was usually done by early afternoon, so I traveled around the island with Eleanor or went to the beach or took my camera on long walks. On days when I was cleaning cars in the sunshine with the radio blaring, I'd laugh to myself about how different this was from my life in New York. It was a peaceful, happy time, and I fell in love with the Vineyard. I do believe that there are very few places where your soul feels comfortable, and I had unexpectedly found mine. By the end of September it was time to go back to New York and start looking for my next job.

A week or so before I was to leave, Eleanor and I went to the farmers market and my life changed. Again. I had my camera slung over my shoulder and was in line to get lemonade. "Are you a photographer?" asked the guy making the lemonade. "Yes," I said, and handed him my new business card, printed on a standard Staples form, stating my name, Photographer, New York/Martha's Vineyard and my cell phone number. "I'm getting married over Columbus Day weekend," he said, adding, "I'm a graphic designer so maybe we can do a trade. I think you need a real business card." And so I started my new career.

Just before going back to New York, Eleanor told me that she and Dave were going to Florida for the winter and needed someone to housesit. I told her I would think about it and left two days later, knowing I would be returning over Columbus Day weekend to shoot the wedding. I returned to the city sadly anticipating having to find a job, not knowing what to expect, and yearning to go back to the Vineyard.

The next day I got on the subway. As I was putting my token into the turnstile, a mass of humanity streamed up the steps from an uptown train and a large man with a screwed-up, unhappy face walked right into me coming through that same turnstile. "That's it," I thought. "I'm moving to Martha's Vineyard." I called my parents and told them this was the one thing that had felt right in 12 years. They agreed, on the condition that I find a good psychiatrist and continue therapy three days a week. As luck would have it, my psychiatrist in New York knew a doctor on the Vineyard.

A NEW LIFE

A couple of weeks later, I took off for the Vineyard. Somewhere I have a photo of me sitting in my U-Haul truck, the first vehicle loaded on to the ferry, a huge smile on my face. This was my decision, my adventure, my life. If it didn't work, I would go home and start all over.

I shot that wedding and started getting others through word of mouth and wedding planners. I made some good friends and I focused on my business. Two months after arriving, I even bought a small house, purchased with money that my father had put aside for me.

During my childhood and after my parents' divorce, one of my favorite things to do was to look through our family photo albums and see the history of my life, of my parents' lives. I was drawn to my profession by my own love of those photographs and by the concept of providing others with documentation of their own family history. And here I was: I had circled around to my dream, though as a portrait and wedding photographer, not as a teacher. I am now going into my 15th season on Martha's Vineyard.

In that time I have lived without the hell of the roller coaster. I've established myself and my business as part of this special community; lived through failed love affairs and feelings in my late 30s that I would never marry; found my soul mate and rejoiced at getting married; lived through my father's death from pancreatic cancer and some incredible family drama. I gradually decreased from three to one therapy sessions per week and now I see the doctor once every two months for medication check-ins. When I have started to feel down, I realize and admit it, and my medication is adjusted.

I was not doomed by my bipolar diagnosis and there are many, like me, who have come to live fulfilled, happy, and peaceful lives with the illness. When I share my story with people, their reaction is "Really?" They have not known me as either depressed or hypomanic, and I do not fit their image of bipolar. I never think of myself as mentally ill. I remember to take a pill every morning and to keep my prescription from running out. It's been 15 years since my last major depression, longer than I spent in the throes of the illness. I know I am never going to feel that horrible again because I am taking care of myself.

In accepting my illness and listening to myself, I found my way back to the inner strength of that little girl who knew that her life was supposed to be good. When I saw myself as a victim,

I was helpless to change my circumstances. I learned that the only person responsible for my happiness is me and I realized that I was capable of changing my life to be what I envisioned: a life full of joy and freedom and possibility. I have been humbled by my struggles of the past. My journey has made me more compassionate, forgiving, and understanding of others' experiences. My husband has helped me to live with a more open heart and more compassion than I ever thought possible, and our love grounds me and inspires me to be a better person. I have found peace. And love. And my true self.

Nicole Friedler Brisson is an acclaimed wedding and portrait photographer (nicolefriedler.com). She grew up in Summit, New Jersey, and graduated from Smith College. After living and working for 10 years in New York City, she moved to Martha's Vineyard. In 2013 she celebrates her 15th year in business living her dream. Nicole has always aspired to be a writer, and now is mining the challenging experiences in her life in the hopes that they may bring comfort and understanding to others. She lives on Martha's Vineyard with her husband, Michael. She can be reached at nicole@nicolefriedler.com.

TAKING CONTROL OF MY FEARFUL LIFE

Step-by-step strategies lead from panic attacks to confidence

Mary Carran Webster

I probably should have told the psychologist what prompted me to seek therapy. But when you think you're going crazy, you do dumb things, like hide your feelings from the person who might be able to steer you to a better place.

Truth is, I was scared.

Strange things had been happening to me for 14 years. Things I didn't understand. Things I couldn't explain. Things I didn't want anyone to know. So as the weeks of therapy rolled into months, my secret remained buried. The psychologist wasn't the only one I fooled. Add my family, friends, co-workers, bosses.

The strangeness started in 1971. A recent graduate of Ohio State University, I decided to take a road trip alone—before starting my first big-girl job in radio—from Columbus, Ohio, to Atlantic City, New Jersey. Less than an hour from the boardwalk, things started to go very wrong.

Suddenly, sweat trickled down my forehead, my mouth became so dry I had trouble swallowing, and my heart raced the way it does when a driver crosses into your lane and spares you from certain death by swerving at the last second. Only no one was in my lane. I steered to the middle of the grassy median and stopped.

What just happened? I decided it wasn't a heart attack, and convinced myself that my body had sensed a mechanical problem and went a little overboard in its drive to get me off the road. I related the bad-car story to the nice patrolman who called for a tow, but the mechanic who spent three days checking fluids and pulling things apart couldn't find a thing wrong with it.

SELF-DEFEATING CHANGES

My broadcast news career took off. I moved from commercial to public radio, where I covered city government and anchored two 20-minute daily newscasts. I was earning respect in a career I loved. But those strange feelings returned again and again. They began to affect how I lived my life.

Exercise was becoming a problem. I'd always been active. I even completed a two-day, 210-mile bike ride in the late '70s and ran a 5K a year later. My heart rate was good. Until it wasn't. Suddenly, just months after crossing the finish line, every time I did any kind of exercise, my chest would hurt. Several trips to the emergency room yielded no bad diagnosis, but the uncomfortable feelings persisted. I was frightened, so I stopped exercising.

I also started to feel so sick while on escalators that I thought I was going to faint, fall, and be swallowed up by the machine that powered them. Shopping in malls became so problematic that sometimes I didn't think I would make it out alive.

Airports, with the long, wide hallways teeming with people,

became another place to fear. I'd be fine at check-in, but on the way to the gate I'd become dizzy and disoriented. Somehow, I'd board the plane. It was so odd, I thought, to be afraid of airports but not of flying.

Going to the grocery store became a challenge. If I ran into a friend, those odd symptoms would envelop me. I often wondered what people thought when I'd try to answer them while sweating and fighting to breathe and swallow. Surely, they must have noticed. Yet no one ever asked if I was okay. I began grocery shopping late at night, when few people were around.

THE ATTACK THAT SCARED ME INTO ACTION

Fast forward to 1983. I was a reporter at Columbus' morning newspaper, the *Citizen-Journal,* where I had worked my way up in less than three years from general assignment to political reporter and columnist. I was working when I suffered my first debilitating episode.

The memory is as clear today as the day it happened. The *C-J's* editor sent me to interview people in the Ohio Department of Insurance. No matter that the only thing I knew about insurance was paying premiums. When I arrived, three people were waiting for me, and they peppered me with questions about the current mayoral campaign before turning to insurance. I asked questions and took notes. The interview developed a sort of rhythm before all hell broke loose.

Sweat percolated up from my feet and slid down my forehead so fast it caught me off guard. My chest felt as if someone was twisting my heart the way you wring water from a washcloth. My mouth was desert dry. I couldn't swallow or catch my breath. The three people blurred into one. I remember hearing them talk, but the words were nonsensical.

I thought I was going to die, and I didn't want to die in a strange room, in a strange building, surrounded by strangers. I mumbled something about not feeling well and fled.

Once outside, I sat on a cement planter to regroup. My hair was soaked, but the sweating had stopped. The chest pain subsided, and my breath came back. After resting for a few minutes, I stood up.

Big mistake! The world started to spin. I grabbed the side of the building. I clutched my chest and fought for air. I was eight blocks away from my car, and I wasn't sure I could make it there.

Still holding onto the building, I inched to the corner. The building ended, and the crosswalk beckoned. I took a step, panicked, backed up, and reached again for the building. Again, I stepped tentatively to the curb. I grasped the arm of a woman, telling her I was dizzy and needed help crossing the street. On the other side, I grabbed the side of the nearest building and started the slow trek to the next intersection. The world was still spinning when I held onto another stranger and made it across another street.

So it went, block by block, until I reached my car. I went immediately to the emergency room. Within minutes, I was hooked up to a heart monitor. Blood was drawn. Questions were asked. An EKG machine appeared.

The ER doctor told me I was going to be okay. My heart rate was elevated when I arrived but had since stabilized; the EKG was normal. To be on the safe side, he attached me to a portable monitor that would register my heartbeats for the next 24 hours. He sent me home.

The next day, I was back at work, where I wrote a brief, not-so-good insurance story. The heart monitor was hard to hide, but I just told people my doctor was running routine tests.

Life was fine for a few weeks, until the next episode, and the one after that.

Finally, I called my parents and told them I was having some problems. I left out most of the details, but they were worried enough to arrange a battery of tests at the Cleveland Clinic, where a cardiologist concluded that my heart was fine. He attributed my episodes to stress and told me they would continue until I made significant changes in my life, starting with my job.

I quit my job at the *C-J* and enrolled in graduate school at Ohio State. I picked up a class to teach, essentially trading one type of stress for another in a less public environment. I still avoided escalators and shopping malls, and food-shopped at night, but for the most part I was episode free.

After completing my course work, I accepted the position of associate editor at *Business First,* a weekly Columbus newspaper. It was an inside job. I didn't have to interview anyone, and for two years I felt pretty good. Until I didn't.

Author Richard Rhodes was coming to town to speak as part of the Thurber Writers' Series, and I was asked to introduce him. He was one of my favorite authors, and I worked for days on the introduction. Hours before the event, I had a series of mini-episodes, and I was afraid that standing in front of Rhodes and 200 people would be disastrous. I called the organizer with some lame excuse about having to work late. Reneging on commitments was nothing new. I'd been doing it for a while, mostly to friends. I let fear guide me and hated myself for it.

EUREKA!

Then one day I learned in the pages of *Lear* magazine that the odd things I'd been experiencing were panic attacks. Putting a name to my problem initially gave me a sense of relief. I wasn't nuts after all.

The minute I finished the article, I phoned the psychologist I had fooled earlier and asked if she knew about panic attacks. She did, and she also knew of an OSU psychiatrist who was conducting clinical trials on Imipramine, a drug that showed promise in treating panic symptoms. The timing was perfect. I was leaving *Business First* to join the OSU School of Journalism as adviser to the student newspaper. The psychiatrist's office was nearby.

Nineteen years after my first episode, I finally knew what was wrong with me, and I was going to get help.

First came the diagnosis: panic anxiety disorder, which is characterized by frequent, recurring panic attacks and often results from a chemical imbalance in the brain. Then came the revelation that I was likely to experience repeated episodes while the dosage of Imipramine rose gradually before leveling off at a predetermined strength.

The doctor wasn't kidding. I would be overcome while teaching class. One day, I literally could not cross the threshold to leave my office. I panicked uncontrollably every time I tried. I had to phone my boyfriend, one of the few people to know of my diagnosis, to help me.

Once the drug reached full strength, I began behavioral therapy. The psychiatrist would assign a task and have me rate the likelihood that I'd complete it, for example, riding the dreaded escalator to the hospital's basement cafeteria, ordering, and eating lunch. I accomplished the tasks, but others in the therapy sessions weren't as fortunate. Some were so afraid that they flat out refused to even start a task. Listening to them made me realize I had a strength deep within me, a strength that would lead me to overcome my fear and the attacks themselves.

I stayed on Imipramine for about a year until the clinical trial ended. The psychiatrist believed the drug would not just treat panic attacks but would eradicate them altogether, rendering the drug unnecessary. When the research showed otherwise, I was shown the door, but not before receiving the names of other psychiatrists who treated my disorder. I was okay with the change.

Once the Imipramine was at full strength, the panic attacks subsided, but the side effects were awful: profuse sweating 24/7, constant tremors, insomnia, sexual dysfunction. When I went off the Imipramine, the attacks started up again.

During the next two years, I experimented with several drugs until I found two with the least objectionable side effects. My new psychiatrist didn't offer behavioral therapy, so I developed my own program. But first I changed jobs again. With my OSU contract ending, I looked for a low-profile job that would afford me the time and atmosphere to begin my healing regimen. I found it as manager of public affairs for the Ohio Crime Victims Compensation Program. It was basically a desk job, out of the spotlight, and with a small staff and deadlines of my choosing.

HOME-GROWN THERAPY

To develop my own program, I began with a simple review of my attack history. I wrote down everything I could remember about every attack. I organized the attacks into two groups: mini and full-blown. Page after page, I relived my nightmarish life. It was hard. It was scary. But in a weird way it was exhilarating because I was determined to take control of my life.

Then it was time to learn what the experts had to say.

Google wasn't around in 1990, so librarians and booksellers were my search engines. Not much had been written about panic anxiety disorder, but I devoured what I could find. I learned that women were more likely targets than men and that the first signs tended to start in our mid-20s, with attacks coming out of nowhere with no advance warning. Symptoms mimic a heart attack, which is why many of us camp out in emergency rooms and why, when told we're okay, we think we're sliding into insanity.

I drew a line down the middle of the pages of a yellow legal pad. On one side, I put what I was doing when an episode occurred and a description of the symptoms. If I was to succeed, I knew I'd need early victories to keep me going, so I listed the mini-attacks as high priorities. On the other side of the paper, I wrote possible strategies for dealing with them.

It was time to act.

The building where I worked was attached to the largest indoor shopping mall in Columbus. In malls I had felt faint, became disoriented, and couldn't breathe, so that's where I started. Because episodes were preceded by dry mouth, I armed myself with a bottle of water and headed to the mall. I took a sip of water as soon as my mouth felt dry, but I began choking as I fought to breathe. It was a disaster.

The next time, I sipped the water before I entered the mall, swallowing all but a small amount, which I swished around as I opened the door. That didn't work either. I stopped breathing, and the water went down the wrong pipe. I coughed. I cried. I fled.

My strategy was flawed. I decided I was trying to conquer too much. I eliminated the places, and from the confines of my home, where I felt safe, I worked on the symptoms. The places would come later during the testing phase.

Hard candy helped me create extra saliva so my mouth couldn't dry up. I bought sugar-free lemon drops by the pound and carried them in my purse and pockets.

I began working on breathing. For weeks, I practiced deep breathing, no matter where I was. Placing my hand on my abdomen, I would take in a big gulp air, push it down until my hand moved, then let it out.

I had read that people with anxiety issues often feared wide open spaces. I wondered if that explained my attacks in malls and at airports. I explored ways to visually shrink space by looking down instead of ahead and by walking close to walls instead of in the middle of hallways.

Always, I reminded myself of two things: I was not going to have a heart attack, and I was not going crazy.

Armed with the knowledge I had gained, I sucked a lemon drop, breathed deeply, and headed once again into the mall. The visit went so well that I began walking through the mall every morning from my car to the office. I wasn't always symptom free, but I was making progress.

Escalators were next. I sucked a piece of candy, breathed deeply and up I went. I practiced going up and down for at least an hour. I wasn't afraid. I didn't panic.

Soon I was offering to pick up friends at the airport. I needed practice shrinking the hallways, and because there were no security stops in those days I could walk to the gates. I began to understand that it wasn't the airport I feared. What I feared was having a panic attack, and I associated them with the airport—and other public places—because that's where they'd occurred. Feeling smart and victorious, I decided it was time to food shop in daylight.

My attacks seem to be triggered when people came up from behind me and started talking. My strategy involved surveying the store when I entered, looking for people I knew. When I spotted someone, I'd go right up to him or her and start talking. By taking the surprise out of the equation, I eliminated the fear.

Exercise posed a different challenge because any time my heart rate started to go up, I'd get scared. Armed with my props and tricks, I worked my way up slowly, first walking, then jogging.

The strategies were working on the mini-attacks, but I needed to know and do more to overcome the full-blown ones. Preparation became a key strategy. I developed a training program for victims' advocates and decided to take it on the road. I started with small groups of advocates I knew and prepared like crazy. I didn't want to be surprised by a question. The strategy worked, the presentation went well, and soon I was speaking to larger groups, and not just to advocates but to county prosecutors and judges.

It took six years to get to this point, and, since I was doing so well, I reduced the dosage of my meds. Another job change also was in the offing. The Ohio attorney general was taking over the compensation program, which meant I had to find work elsewhere.

Elsewhere turned out to be at City Hall. There was a new mayor in town, Michael B. Coleman. I liked him, his politics, his ideas, and the interview with him must have gone well because I was hired as assistant director of the Public Service Department.

The job mainly involved communicating with the public at neighborhood meetings and through the media, thrusting me back into the spotlight I had been running from for 17 years. I missed the action, but was I taking on too much?

Sticking to my preparation strategy, I immersed myself in the functions of the department's five divisions. I got to know the people who worked there—snow plow drivers, trash collectors, janitors, secretaries, engineers, administrators. And I studied the issues likely to come under public scrutiny. I attended community meetings and built relationships with reporters.

The strategy served me well. I no longer sucked on lemon drops. I still practiced breathing, but didn't have to remind myself to breathe. I shopped where I wanted when I wanted. I traveled to Hong Kong, China, and Thailand. I began to share my secret with others. And again I dialed back my meds until I was taking the lowest dosage available.

In my nine years at City Hall, I gave more than a thousand interviews to TV, print, and radio reporters. I gave speeches and guest lectured. I knocked on doors during campaign season. I engaged people who stopped me to compliment the mayor or complain about snow removal.

Not once did I panic!

Was I cured? Yes and no. The diagnosis of panic anxiety disorder still stands, but I no longer suffer the scary, debilitating, and embarrassing symptoms of the past. My strategy works. I am in control, and recently I even began helping others conquer their panic demons in the hopes that they, like me, will achieve success and finally feel at peace.

Life is good.

Mary Carran Webster left City Hall and Columbus in 2009 to spend time with her then 85-year-old mother. She writes and volunteers on several committees in Chagrin Falls, Ohio. She has been free of panic symptoms for 18 years. She dedicates her story to Debbie Phillips and Kacy Cook, whom she fooled while the three worked together at the *Citizen-Journal*, and to her nephew, Jackson Webster, who wanted a book but gets a chapter instead. Mary can be reached at mcwebster7@gmail.com.

PART THREE:
SUPPORT

THROUGH THE FIRE

One woman's story of addiction and recovery

Jenifer Madson

There I was, 21 years old, in some stranger's apartment at 2 a.m., on all fours, drunkenly clawing through the shag carpet for crumbs of cocaine that had fallen when "Mr. Right Now" got up in a huff and knocked it off the table as he stomped out of the room. I snorted everything from that carpet that looked remotely like the drug I craved more than life itself, on a complete tear, until this man finally dragged me off the floor and back to the couch, where I sat panting and wild-eyed, my heart beating out of my chest as I tried to figure out where he was hiding the rest of his stash.

I wish I could tell you that some out-of-body experience that night helped me see how pathetic and desperate I was, but I can't. It wasn't even the worst night I'd ever had. It was just another Saturday night in the life of a cocaine addict and alcoholic.

There was no part of me then that said, "I really should stop this craziness."

Nor were there any rational thoughts of change the morning after I was so drunk that I fell over a toy poodle in someone's kitchen, landing face first on the stone tile floor. I was knocked unconscious and my eyes were blackened for two weeks. I just told myself that was what dark sunglasses were for.

Unfortunately, I could go on and on with similar stories of shame. Suffice it to say that I suffered ever greater humiliation at the hands of my addiction for another three years before I finally got clean and sober. And recovery didn't come from some enlightened conviction of my own; it was a divine concert of grace and opportunity that led me to it. I finally and simply (but not easily) became willing to be led away from the particular hell that my life had become.

AN ADDICTIVE PERSONALITY

My drinking started at the age of 13. I didn't get drunk the first time, but the addictive thinking was present from the start. A group of older friends had invited me to cut out on our church youth group and go with them to eat pizza and drink beer. I was only in middle school and they were in high school, so I felt very grown up to be asked.

As soon as we were in the car, I saw that they had already gotten the beer, and I started doing what I now call "alcoholic math," which was to think, "There are four of us and six beers, so if they each have one, I can have three."

I had never even had a beer before then.

But that incident fairly well characterized the next 10 years: wanting desperately to fit in, I would say or do whatever it took to get what I wanted, which was usually more than my fair share of whatever substance was available.

I controlled my drinking for the next year, only sneaking my parents' liquor or beer, until I started high school. Then I started skipping school to go drink mini bottles of alcohol or wine coolers or whatever my older friends could get away with buying or stealing. It wasn't hard to get alcohol; it was just hard to hide what I was doing. My father was a very high profile teacher at our high school in Naples, Florida, which meant I had to work overtime to sneak a drink.

All this time, I was pursuing a dance career. I had been dancing since I was five years old, and by the time I was in middle school, I decided I wanted to do it professionally, even though I knew I would have to work harder than the girls for whom it seemed so easy. I had a talent for dance, but not really a gift for it.

But I had wonderful dance teachers who encouraged me to pursue this talent, and to add acting and singing to the mix so I could be a "triple threat" on Broadway. And I believed them when they told me I was good enough to make it on Broadway, and I really, really loved the attention I got from being onstage.

So I kept my sights on dancing in New York City, and sure enough, the summer after my freshman year of high school, I was chosen to study dance at the American Ballet Theater school. I studied there for a month, going back and forth between my apartment and the studio for classes, an experience that made me feel very worldly and important.

I shelved the drinking completely while I was there, but no sooner was I back in Naples than I ramped it back up. I also started smoking marijuana.

I was 15 at this time, working at a restaurant and hanging out with people much older than I, and by "hanging out," I mean drinking and getting high with them. The drinking age was 18, so it was really easy to get served in our local bars, something I took advantage of as often as I could.

ONE STEP AHEAD OF TROUBLE

I didn't experience any hugely negative results from drinking or doing drugs at this point; what was escalating was the frequency of use, not the consequences. I kept showing up for school (though my grades were subpar), and for dance classes (although I wasn't often chosen for solos), and for work (where my behavior fell in with everyone else's). My parents were too busy wrestling with a failing marriage to notice what I was up to, so I typically stayed one step ahead of any real trouble.

By my junior year, I had started doing cocaine, not in great quantities—it was pretty expensive, after all—but enough to discover that I loved the confidence it seemed to provide, confidence I never really felt inside.

As talented as I was, and as popular as I seemed to be, nothing felt easy or natural or right. I didn't date—the boys were all too afraid of my dad—so I was just the party girl the boys would hang around, the "make out with today, ignore tomorrow, no one needs to know" girl. I had very few close friends, except the ones who partied like I did, who I chose so I could justify my own habits. Everyone else was either someone to pity, because they couldn't keep up with me and my gang, or someone to be jealous of, because they made things look so much easier than anything ever felt for me. I was constantly lonely and afraid, and alcohol and drugs eased that for me.

I went back to New York City to study dance the summer before my senior year, but instead of focusing on my classes, I spent the better part of it partying in Greenwich Village with friends who were already in college there.

It was the summer I fell in love for the first time, with a boy who was four years older. He was attending film school at New York University, and talked constantly about his dreams of fame and fortune in the film world. He was kind and mischievous, tall and lanky, with wild, curly, strawberry-blond hair. Every time I was with him, I felt hopeful and energized, that I could make it as a dancer in New York, that everything would be okay, that I was someone special. He didn't mind that I was only 16. He simply swept me up for that short time, and then let me go when it was time for me to return home, where I went right back to the mediocre effort I put into everything except drinking and using drugs.

My senior year was a disaster. My parents' marriage was falling apart, and I was spending more and more time partying with my friends, and less and less time training—although I would tell anyone who would listen how I was going to go be a Broadway star.

By this time, I was using just about any drug I could get. On any given weekend, I could be found with amphetamines, barbiturates, marijuana, cocaine, PCP, hallucinogenic mushrooms— you name it and I was probably trying it.

Right after high school, I entered the University of South Florida as a dance major. It was my first time away from home for an extended time, and once there, my addiction hit full speed. There was no person, no place, no thing to stop me from drinking and using whenever, whatever, and however I wanted. All bets were off on what morals I would compromise to get the drugs and alcohol I now needed day and night to function.

It wasn't long before I was on academic probation because I barely showed up for my classes, and when I did, I was either strung out on speed in the morning to help my hangover, or half drunk on beer in the afternoon, on my way to harder liquor at night. I began to hate my dance classes—the thing I had loved more than anything—because of how they interfered with my addictions.

But I wasn't ready to kill the dream yet, not consciously anyway. After a year of college, I went back home, determined to figure out how to become a professional dancer. While in Naples, I won a spot in the cast of a traveling production of Cabaret, earned my Actor's Equity card, and finally gained status as a professional dancer.

Shortly after the show ended in Florida, I moved to New York. I had friends waiting for me when I arrived—the dancers from the show, my friend Kerry from home, even my dear first love from that summer in high school.

I started tending bar at night, auditioning by day, and drinking and drugging through it all. I lied to, stole from, and cheated my bosses and friends to maintain my habits. I still called myself a dancer because I would catch an audition here and there—and even get callbacks—but I never made the cut. I was pissed off and bitter most of the time, chalking up my disappointments to everyone else's lack of understanding or vision.

LOST IN THE HAZE
OF ADDICTION

I was "that girl," the one who was always someplace doing something I should appreciate more than I was able to, in great cities, with great people and great opportunities, all of which got lost in the haze of my addiction. My disease prevented me from ever allowing myself to be good enough—as a dancer, a girlfriend, a daughter, a sister, or as a friend. About a year after I moved to New York, I slunk back to Naples and settled into a life where I traded every value I had to satisfy my addictions, and the worst part was, if I even knew I needed help, I still wasn't ready to ask for it.

My dance career was over before it had even begun.

My education had been traded for my delusions.

My relationships were torched.

I had gone from a bright, intelligent, and social young girl to a desperate, lonely, sick and tired young woman, with no prospects for a meaningful life on any level.

And I still wasn't done.

Fast-forward through the experience that opened this chapter, and I finally returned to college on my parents' strong recommendation, this time in South Carolina. They could finally see how bad things had gotten for me and assumed that, if I got away from the "bad elements" in my hometown, I would get better.

The problem was that I went with me. And soon after I arrived, I was back to working 24 hours a day to maintain my habits.

About four months after I arrived at school, following a particularly heavy night of drinking and using, I woke up vomiting, shaking, and crying, as physically and emotionally sick as I had ever felt in my life. I picked up the phone and called my mother.

My mom had gotten sober the year before, after a 30-day stint in rehab to address the alcoholism that had severely escalated for her in a few short years following her divorce from my dad. I lived—and drank—with her during those years, and when she went to treatment, I could only see her alcoholism, not my own. I visited her in treatment about 20 days into her stay, and when she walked out to greet me, she looked more beautiful and healthy than I had ever remembered. I couldn't reconcile how she looked so wonderful but had to stay, while I felt like total shit but was free to leave. She left treatment about two weeks later and hasn't had a drink since.

So on that fateful morning a year later, I called to tell her that my friends drank too much and that I didn't want to drink anymore. She listened patiently, and even though she knew the disease was mine to confront, she suggested I look into Al-Anon, to understand why my friends and family drank the way they did. I rushed off the phone with her to find an Al-Anon meeting, convinced that if I could figure out everyone else's problems, I would be okay.

Mom was pretty sneaky in that conversation, knowing that, if she came right out and told me to get help for my own drinking, I would be too stubborn and prideful to hear it. In the meantime, she mailed me a pamphlet titled "Young People in AA," which showed up at my dorm about three days later. I opened her letter and read the brochure, which listed about 20 questions that would indicate whether someone had a problem with alcohol. I read them and answered "yes" to each one, I cried my eyes out as I realized that I was the one who needed help.

So I called the same number I had for the Al-Anon meeting, even got the same guy on the phone, and told him I needed an AA meeting. He told me to come to the same place he had mentioned before, that coming Friday, but to come an hour earlier.

Two days later, I went to my first meeting, shaking and crying so hard I could barely hold the cup of coffee these patient, loving strangers offered me as they led me to a chair.

The only thing I remember from that meeting was the sign on the wall that read, "You never have to be alone again," which I was convinced would be true for everyone except me. But I stayed anyway, and came back for as many meetings as I could to keep from being alone with my anxiety and fear.

FINDING JOY AND LOVE AND PURPOSE

Over time, through countless hours of doing the work of understanding the disease of addiction—looking at my past, taking responsibility for my part in it, and making amends for it—my life turned from a constant horror into one of joy and love and purpose. The people who guided me in my recovery were relentless in their belief that I was worth saving and, eventually, I came to believe it as well.

I did my part by accepting their support and following their simple suggestions: take things "one day at a time," "let go and let God," and a hundred others just like these. I couldn't ignore the progress I saw in their lives from following these directions, so I followed them too, day in and day out, in good times and bad. Then one day I looked up and realized that I felt a happiness and a freedom I had never imagined was possible.

I have not had a drink or a drug since the day of that first meeting, which is proof that miracles happen.

And while my life has not been perfect in sobriety, I have experienced it fully—from excruciating pain to extraordinary joy—without the need for alcohol or drugs to either numb the pain or "enhance" the celebration. I not only got my life back, I got it in 3-D Technicolor.

Now, when I dance, it is joyful and free, as I am.

Now, more than 27 years since I attended that first meeting, my life is peaceful, fulfilling, and full of joy. In that time, I have owned and run multi-million dollar companies, become a published author, developed deeply satisfying relationships with my friends and family, and given back to my community as a mentor to at-risk youth, entrepreneurs, and people in recovery.

Nothing about my life before recovery pointed to these possibilities. Nor was I able early in sobriety to dream about my future; I just wanted to get away from who I was and what I had done. But by the grace of some spiritual power, once on the path to recovery, I had people every step of the way who saw more for me than I could for myself, who loved me until I could love myself. Soon, their promise of a new freedom and a new happiness started to come true.

What my sobriety has taught me is this: We will rarely choose what is practical, or a "should"; we shift and accomplish great things in our life when some social, physical, moral, or spiritual imperative has dictated that we must.

My "musts" have changed. They have gone from "must stop puking, shaking, and crying" to "must grow and serve others"; my results in life have been reshaped accordingly. I figured out the things I must do, the person I must be, the ways in which I must serve, in all areas of my life. By letting these drive me and allowing others who have overcome the same struggles guide me, my life has unfolded in miraculous ways.

Jenifer Madson is an award-winning author, speaker, and success coach whose journey in recovery has informed every aspect of her work in the personal development field. She uses lessons from her unique story of redemption to help people from all walks of life— from at-risk youth to Fortune 100 executives—awaken to their highest potential. Her newest book, *Living The Promises,* can be found at www.jenifermadson.com. When she's not working, she can be found in the dance studio or in a 12-step meeting.

VOICE LESSONS

Learning to speak up for myself and others

Linda Neff

Fifty years is a long time to find your voice. I know now that mine has always been with me, but I was slow to believe and recognize it. Not trusting my ability to articulate my value system, I was hesitant to speak up and speak out for justice and equality for all people.

Fortunately, all my life, I've had inspiring people supporting me in my search—my parents, sister, teachers, faith leaders, husband, daughter, and gal pals. One of my trusted mentors shared this adage: "The teacher appears when the student is ready." We often don't hear a message, she said, despite it being shared over and over because we're not ready to receive the lesson. Until recently, I'd been a reluctant student, mostly thanks to my extreme distaste for confrontation. Faced with conflict, my palms and pits would sweat profusely. More often than not, I'd then retreat into silence.

FIRST WHISPERS

Along the way, the teacher appeared frequently, although I didn't recognize the lessons until much later. One of my first recollections of admiring others' abilities to assert themselves happened the night my sister was born. I was not quite four-years old. My father, dressed in a suit, took me to see *Mary Poppins*—still one of my favorite movies. I remember how special I felt. I wore an empire-waist dress with a satin bow, lace tights, patent leather shoes, and a matching hat and a muff. While I loved everything about the movie, what stood out most and has remained with me were Mrs. Banks singing her impassioned "Sister Suffragette" and Michael Banks wanting to give his tuppence to the bird lady, against the advice of a bunch of crusty, petulant white men. I saw them both as being brave, standing up for what they believed in.

I recall my parents offering emotional support and friendship to a young man my father worked with; he was an Air Force pilot who flew one of the last flights out of Vietnam. I have a poignant memory of him standing in my parents' kitchen, sharing the story of his last flight. He began sobbing, and my father wrapped him in a comforting bear hug as my mother rubbed his back. I felt a deep sadness and thought about how brave he was and how scared he must have been. There were people hanging on to his aircraft as he was taking off; some didn't make it out. Were there children among them? How could the land of the free and the home of the brave leave so many behind? Why wasn't our great country and President Nixon doing something to help? I was 13 years old, and my voice was whispering to me inside, but I still could not make it heard to others.

In high school, the debate team captivated me. Most intriguing were the shoeboxes they toted between debate competitions, brimming with 3x5 index cards covered with facts. The debaters' ability to quickly retrieve the exact card they needed was impressive. But it was their aggressive defense of their positions that really got my attention. Even as their shouts and interruptions made me want to sprint away, I had the deepest respect for their capacity to use their voices and intellects in the moment. While I coveted those shoeboxes and all they represented, the student in me avoided the lesson on using facts and words to change and inform minds.

My first week attending Purdue University in 1979 was an eye-opener. A cross was burned in the front yard of a black fraternity. Where were the protests? Where was the outrage? I lived in an identity that was privileged but precarious. This privilege held me back from speaking out about something I knew was fundamentally wrong. My voice was telling me to do something. Instead, I went to class.

TUNING IN TO CAREER

Growing up in the 1960s and '70s, I was aware of the women's movement—women striving to give future generations equal rights and better opportunities for workplace advancement. They did the difficult work. Now it was up to me and my generation to advance it through a strong commitment to our professions.

In 1985, I threw myself into a career in marketing communications and advertising, an industry dominated by men. To break in, I took a job as an administrative assistant working on a car account. I looked for ways to provide value outside of my defined role. When a junior account executive position was established, I wanted it. But the job was given to a young man with no prior experience; I wasn't even considered for an interview. I was devastated—and furious. I wrote a letter to my boss's boss (oh, to be young again!) decrying the unfairness of the situation and citing my achievements and stellar performance appraisals. In response, I received a severe reprimand from the boss of my boss's boss: "Who do you think you are?" he demanded. "Clearly you don't understand your place." I was so overwhelmed by the shouting and verbal battery that I nearly fainted during the meeting. I had tested my voice and then froze in fear when I was called on to defend it. The controversy was more than I could handle, but—as I realized only in hindsight—I managed a step forward: I resigned.

I beat myself up for weeks afterward, and it took time to rebound. I finally realized I had done the strong thing by standing up for myself. I became more determined than ever to make my way. I started to believe that, if I stayed true to my voice, my fear of conflict could become less intimidating while the opportunities would be more exciting.

Exciting they were. One promotion led to another, and eventually, I led a profitable business unit in a global marketing communications and advertising organization. I advocated for good work that would drive business results for my clients and reflect well on our team. I became more confident in my own skills and my abilities as a big-picture, creative, and strategic thinker who could push the boundaries to drive an exceptional work product.

Whether or not I recognized it at the time, my voice was emerging; I began to trust it more and more. I had even learned to get through the occasional shouting battles. I was making progress.

During this time I also met my future husband, Chuck. It was one of the biggest—and happiest—shocks of my life. I'd long since decided I'd never marry. We worked together to manage two thriving careers, especially after the birth of our daughter, Helen, in 1998.

For 20 years, I loved my job and my colleagues, but I became exhausted. My highly evolved skills of navigating airport security and preparing late night presentations in hotel rooms followed by early morning presentations came at a price. They were the trade-off to spontaneous mini-golf excursions, dinners around the kitchen table and grade school performances with my husband and our beautiful daughter. When the economy shifted, I had an opportunity to accept a package to leave my position. I left the career I loved to focus on the things that meant the most to me: my husband, my daughter, and myself.

Not quite a year into my blissful stay-at-home status, my friend Edie called. She is a tireless advocate for women, and I thought she was calling to ask me to volunteer for something. Much to my surprise, Edie wanted me to interview for a job. And not just any job. It was to lead the fundraising and communications departments of a non-profit reproductive healthcare provider. The job would not be merely challenging; it was a lightning rod for social and political conflict.

VOICING CONFLICT: FROM TWEETS TO CHANTS

True, I had been supporting this organization since college, even when money was tight. But did Edie know she was calling a person who despised conflict? Beads of sweat began forming in my palms. I begged off, telling her I wasn't the right person for the job. Instead, I recommended my friend Sharon, an articulate, dynamic woman who is not afraid of controversy. Sharon secured an interview right away.

A few days later, my doorbell rang. There was Sharon, fresh from the interview. I answered the door with a big smile, fully expecting to hear about her new job. Without even a hello, she assailed me, "Neff, I don't know what the hell your problem is. This job is yours, not mine!" For the next two hours, Sharon sat with me, as a good friend will do, and annihilated every barrier I threw up as to why she was wrong.

Finally, with my heart pounding and a knotted stomach, I mustered the courage to call Edie. "I'll interview for the job," I told her.

After a rigorous interview process, I got the position. I was in that proverbial barrel, lid shut tight, ready to plummet down the waterfall. Was I ready for this? Did I have what it was going to take? How would I deal with the protestors hurling insults— those hateful zealots whose purpose was to deny women access to essential healthcare? Would my family be safe? I had so many doubts.

In reality, this step was inevitable. A theme of social justice, especially the women's and civil rights movements, was woven throughout my adolescent and adult life. I had grown up with a support system that prepared me to give voice to the issues that mattered to me. I had strong female role models, women who moved with grace and confidence. My parents told my sister and me that we could do anything, and for the most part we believed them.

While I stretched myself to create a successful career, I also used that career as a cover to avoid fully committing to the things I believed in. I was wrapped up in my work, too busy to address social inequities hands-on. So I sent money.

All of that was about to change.

In September 2009, as I arrived for the first day of my new job, I decided that the protestors surrounding the entrance would not deter me. As I got closer to the front door of the building, I remembered my mother's words: "We are all God's children." As the people on the sidewalk glared and shouted at me, I responded with a sincere, "Good morning." They were praying for me. That's nice! Who doesn't need an extra prayer to get their day started, especially when you've already picked out your new first-day-on-the-job outfit?

Just as I had thrown myself into my for-profit career, I was determined to do the same with my new non-profit career. In my previous work, we learned as much as we could about our clients and their business through hands-on immersion (including my most spectacular immersion—spending a week at boot camp with the U.S. Army). I began looking for those kinds of openings. Besides, it kept me from thinking about those people shouting on the sidewalk.

Within the first few months, I learned about an opportunity to immerse myself in the advocacy aspect of the organization. A group of co-workers and supporters were going to Washington, D.C., for a lobby day. This was perfect. I was a veteran traveler, so a 24-hour trip was no big deal. The only difference from my other experiences was that I would be traveling on a bus. No airline club? No five-star accommodations? I wanted to retreat. Fortunately, the voice in my head spoke up: "Excuse me. This is what you're all about. Put on your big-girl pants, slap on some lipstick, and get on that bus before it leaves without you."

Pulling my Hartmann roller board and wearing my signature pearls and a fabulous pair of Prada shoes, I boarded what appeared to be a vintage (code for old, musty and broken-down) Greyhound bus. My outfit was a bit out of place, but we were a diverse group of traveling companions who shared a common purpose. We were all there to advocate for women, and more specifically to speak out against the Stupak Amendment, which was designed to effectively ban coverage for most abortion care as part of health-care reform. (The amendment ultimately passed and was seen as a loss by both pro-choice and pro-life proponents.) As the bus rolled along on that early December evening, I leaned into this immersion adventure, and I began using my voice—140 characters at a time:

- My toe-in-the-water Tweet: On DC bound Greyhound to #stopstupak
- My voice gaining confidence Tweet: DC Bound #StopStupak Rally Bus on outskirts of DC. Mr Stupak we need to talk!
- My no-turning-back Tweet: Ready to talk #StopStupak with legislators and thank Kind and Feingold for their support.

After traveling through the night from Milwaukee, I stepped off the bus a little before 8 a.m. in Washington, D.C. Someone suddenly slapped a sticker on me. It said, "This is what a feminist looks like." This is what a *what* looks like? I remember the physicality of that moment. I stood a little straighter and moved the sticker to a place of prominence on the left lapel of my jacket. Yes, indeed! This *is* what a feminist looks like, and I've got something to say! And then I knew that the teacher had appeared as I fully grasped the lesson of using my own voice to create change.

I moved through that lobby day—yes, I did have sweaty pits and palms, but I was making progress—and my self-assurance began to grow. I heard strong women speak that day—Planned Parenthood Federation of America President Cecile Richards, Senator Barbara Boxer, Congresswoman Carolyn Maloney—all wanting to make sure that women would not be worse off after healthcare reform.

A year or so after that trip, Wisconsin became the center of a national dialogue regarding unions, collective bargaining, and healthcare. Our newly elected governor, Scott Walker, introduced legislation that would eliminate workers' rights and restrict health-care access for those of lesser means. In the bitter cold of our Wisconsin winter, we packed up our family, weekend after weekend, and joined the protests. It was too important to be quiet. Our homemade sign read: "Pro Union, Pro BadgerCare, Pro Family! Kill the Bill!" We marched around the capital with thousands of others, chanting, "This is what democracy looks like." I even pulled out my cowbell from my college football days. The protests and the chants helped bolster my commitment.

The more experiences I had, the more comfortable I became engaging in conversation about my value system. I didn't shy away from people I knew had different values than mine, even when some of them de-friended me on Facebook, saying I was embarrassing.

But then, as my advocacy became more conspicuous, I got spooked. The protestors learned my name. They began mocking me and getting as close as they could and whispering in my ear, "Good morning, Linda Neff." And then someone placed a single pink knitting needle in our front yard. Could I still really do this job? Were my husband and daughter safe? How far would the haters go?

I began wearing my sunglasses, even on the darkest days, as a form of armor to shield myself from the taunts and jeers. My confidence was waning. Those who wished to deny women access to essential healthcare were winning out.

On one particular day, the protestors were especially nasty. I was moving quickly, too quickly. I pulled the metal bottom of the heavy front door across the top of my foot. Despite my thick leather winter boot, I cut the top of my foot and severely bruised my toes. I limped to the bathroom stall so others wouldn't see me crying. And how was it that I thought I could do this job?

In an effort to buoy my spirits, a work friend advised me to avoid the whole protest scene and start coming in through the back door. Hmmm, the back door! Oh, thank goodness, I thought, I can use the back door. It brought relief.

And then there was that voice inside of me, the same one that told me to get on the bus. The back door? Was I only willing to walk a little way on this path and then stop? In the end, did I truly not have the courage of my convictions? What behavior did I want to model for my daughter and other women? Was I someone who confidently entered through the front entrance, or would I choose to duck in the back door?

I knew what it looked like to take the back door. It looked like not questioning why the United States left Vietnamese families and children behind. It looked like going to class instead of speaking out against an outrageous cross-burning in front of a black fraternity. It looked like sending money instead of getting involved.

It was a stunning moment of clarity, as I experienced the teacher and my inner voice meld into one. The courage of conviction had always been there. The belief in equality and fairness were always present. The missing link was trust.

I was now fully aware of my voice. I knew I was ready to model Mrs. Banks and her son Michael, standing up for what they believed in. I knew I wanted to model that same courageousness for my own daughter. There really wasn't much to decide or even think about. I knew the answer before it was asked.

I stood a little taller and walked with purpose and conviction—through the same door that welcomes women in search of access to annual exams, birth control, cancer screenings, education, and abortion care.

While the path I've chosen isn't always easy or popular, it's the path that allows me to help others find their voices while I continue to develop mine. It's the path that implores me to hold my head high every morning and walk through the gauntlet of individuals who wish to deny women access to essential, life-saving healthcare. It's the path where walking through the front door says every woman matters. I'm unequivocally a woman who walks through the front door, one who has learned to use her voice in support of her beliefs. And for that I'm grateful.

Linda Neff believes in the power of sharing our collective voices and stories to advocate for change in the world, especially as it relates to women, girls, and families. As Linda transitioned to the non-profit world from corporate America's singular focus on accruing wealth, she learned that her greatest currency was her own voice. Linda was raised in the Midwest and now lives in Shorewood, Wisconsin, with her husband and 15-year old daughter, who is the reason for Linda continuing to fine-tune her voice. You can reach Linda at voicesofpearls@gmail.com. Visit her blog at voicesofpearls.wordpress.com and follow her on twitter @MaxPaige.

TOUCHED BY SUICIDE

A sister's journey of grief, guilt, and shame

Tricia Simpson

Bitter, freezing, shivering cold. That is what I remember feeling for a long time after I found out my brother had died. My sweetheart of a little brother, whom I loved with everything I had through more ups and downs than anyone should have to endure, was gone.

Tuesday, December 14, 2004. I was driving to my in-laws' house, where I was staying while my new husband, Dave, and I were in the process of moving from Columbus to San Francisco. Dave was already in California, while I remained to sell our home and wrap up our lives in Ohio.

I called Dave and we talked excitedly about the life changes coming our way. My co-workers were throwing me a going-away party, and Dave would be in Columbus a couple days later. Right after Christmas, we'd jump on a plane and start our new life.

As I entered my in-laws' house, I smelled pizzelles, the traditional Italian waffle cookies. I went to the kitchen to compliment my father-in-law on his baking, but before I had even removed my coat, he gave me a hug. He probably wanted to ensure he was holding on to me for what came next.

"Your brother is gone, Tricia," he told me. "Greg committed suicide. He's dead."

My knees buckled, and I thought I was going to throw up. My father-in-law guided me into the living room where I slumped to the couch.

It is odd that in a moment when my life became one big blur of confusion and grief, I also felt clarity. I didn't yet know how drastically my life would change. But I knew that, from then on, if you looked at the continuum of my life, it would be rooted in the "befores" and "afters" of that day.

I had been through traumatic deaths before. Two young cousins died in drunk driving accidents only a few months apart, my godmother passed away from chronic alcoholism, and my mom's long-term significant other died of a heart attack. All too young. All tragic. Yet, I always bounced back. I was a strong, resilient person before Greg's death. But after he died, I was weak, shaken, broken.

OUR YOUNG LIVES

I was three years old when Greg was born. He became my own live baby doll. I loved having a little brother to hold, feed, and snuggle with. I took on the motherly role that big sisters sometimes do.

Only a year after Greg was born our parents divorced, which drew us even closer to one each other. He and I were best buddies, confidants, despite the fact that we were opposites in many ways. He was hilarious, where I was serious. He was impulsive; I was hesitant to do anything unexpected. He made me more fun, and I helped him understand it was okay to be reflective at times.

Most of my happiest childhood memories involve him: Saturday morning cartoons, foot wars on the couch, neighborhood kickball games, summertime at the pool, beach vacations, dinnertime jokes that drove Mom crazy, and pranking people on the phone, pre-caller ID, of course. And he made the best chocolate cakes from scratch.

One of the harshest realizations after losing him was that I also lost all of the memories that he held close to his heart. The ones he used to remind me of because they were at the surface of his mind but were buried deep in mine. Now I have my memories, but I don't have his. He was the other half to my childhood, and knowing that his memories are buried with him is still difficult for me.

THE PERFECT STORM

August 28, 1994. On the day Greg purchased his first bag of drugs, I'm sure he was just curious, wanting to experiment by smoking a little pot.

But Greg wasn't like most people. He became addicted to drugs the first time he did them. Some people say addiction stems from something in the brain; others believe it's because someone is weak and can't control his behaviors. I believe that when a certain set of circumstances collide, addiction becomes more likely. Yes, there's a chemical imbalance. But life events enable some to overcome addiction, while for others it may be too much to resist. Greg's life set up a perfect storm.

As was often the case with divorced parents in the early 1980s, he and I lived with our mom and visited our dad every other weekend. So we grew up in a household without a consistent male role model. This was a greater danger for Greg because he was repeatedly molested by our paternal grandfather, who threatened to kill our mother if Greg told. The silence led to shame and the shame led to destruction. As frequently happens with those who endure such abuse, Greg suffered from anxiety and depression. It is a vicious cycle, and Greg's life was a textbook example of what can happen when an unfortunate set of circumstances collide.

And collide they did.

Within six months of smoking pot for the first time, he began using every drug he could get his hands on, skipping school, stealing, and lying. He also attempted suicide for the first time. Because of his rapid descent into drugs, my parents quickly jumped into action and found the best rehabilitation center available. Our family was committed to helping him through this treacherous time.

He lived away in the beginning, but later earned the privilege of coming home to sleep. Our house became like a fortress: locks on windows, deadbolts on doors, no television or radio, no newspapers, and an alarm on the bedroom door where Greg and his friends from rehab who accompanied him slept.

The whole family made changes to be part of Greg's healing. I came home from college most weekends to attend Friday Family Night meetings. Our half-sister Jennifer skipped social events, and our parents put their lives on hold to help Greg.

Ironically, some of my happiest memories of Greg from when he was older are from the evenings he'd come home with other boys from rehab. We'd order pizza, play board games, and laugh and have fun. What I remember most is that the other boys were such good guys, just like Greg. They were also addicts.

When Greg and I reviewed his nightly journals, I began to understand the loneliness and shame that he felt about his addiction. Although I was still proud of who he was and believed in him, he had no self-esteem and was disgusted with himself over the things he had done. I still saw a caring, gentle soul, but he couldn't reconcile this with the liar, thief, and addict he'd become.

He was a fighter, though, and at age 18, left rehab sober, happy, and with a new outlook on life. He had a job and a girlfriend and began attending college. That meant that our family was relaxed and happy too. We could exhale; we could live our own lives again.

Then Greg tried heroin. Heroin numbs. It makes you forget. Kids who were sexually abused often turn to the drug for this reason. Heroin and my brother proved to be a deadly combination.

The next five years went something like this: Greg relapses, we panic, Greg runs away, we worry, Greg steals from us or others, we get angry, Greg gets busted, we beg the judge to send him to rehab rather than jail, Greg gets court-ordered to rehab, Greg gets better for a short time, Greg relapses or ODs or runs away from rehab, we panic, Greg gets picked up for other drug-related charges, we feel relief, Greg gets sent back to rehab...and on and on.

Our family camaraderie deteriorated during this time. We were all exhausted. Mom and Dad became divided over how to respond to the constant upheaval. But the sad fact was that, because Greg was 18, there was really nothing we could do. We all tried to control something that wasn't within our power to control.

Then one day, Greg stood in front of a judge and didn't get sent to rehab. He had stolen a check, written it out to himself, and cashed it. He was sentenced to nine years in an Ohio state prison. The judge looked straight into my brother's eyes and said, "And you will not do well in there."

Prison? I couldn't wrap my head around it. I was panicked for my brother who was 5-foot-8, non-violent, non-confrontational, and definitely not a hardcore criminal. For the first couple of years, I made myself believe that there was no difference between a county jail and a state prison. I made myself think that he was okay, spending his days taking classes and staying out of trouble. He sheltered me from knowing more.

I visited him only once. Seeing him in prison was extremely emotional for me. But I held it together while I was with him, trying to ignore the leering looks and sexual invitations from other prisoners. I never went again. It was a purely selfish decision on my part. I could not handle it. In my mind, he was different than every other person there. But the sad reality is that many addicts who come from caring families are thrown into prison instead of rehabilitation.

This is when my own personal secrecy and shame began. I created a system in my mind of who could know what about my family. If you were a best friend who I completely trusted, you would know that he was in jail—not prison—but not much else. If you were a friend who knew my family, you knew that he was in and out of rehab. If you were just an acquaintance, you were definitely kept in the dark. Now it was me who couldn't reconcile the facts of what was going on in what I believed was a "normal" family.

Aside from needing to step off the emotional roller coaster, the shame I felt kept me from being there for him in the same way that I had been when he was in rehab.

The last time I spoke to him was Thanksgiving weekend in 2004. Greg called collect, as he had to, from prison. I am grateful that I agreed to talk with him; I almost didn't. I usually found that talking to him only made it hurt worse. But that night, we talked. And we had the best 15-minute conversation we'd had in a long time. When the one-minute warning came, I remember thinking, "Just ask him to call right back." But I didn't ask. Instead, I said, "I love you so much and I miss you tons." He said the same, and we agreed to talk again soon. I promised to visit him before Christmas. I cried my heart out that night, letting myself feel how much I missed him, how sad I was for his precious life turning out like this.

On December 14, around 4 p.m., Greg's lifeless body was found hanging in his cell. His struggles, disappointments, pain and anguish were all over. He was at peace.

And a new hell began for me.

ALONE IN GRIEF

I remember feeling bitterly cold, but oddly it was from the inside out. I would wake in the mornings and have maybe 30 seconds of calm before the horrific reality washed over me again. Day turned to night and then back to daytime, with minimal, restless sleep. I was in traumatic shock, and it took a long time to come out of it. The entire first year after he was gone is like a black, gaping hole for me. So much of my life changed in that time, but I can't remember it. What I do remember is the guilt, the anguish, thinking it would never end, and feeling completely isolated from the rest of the world. I thought nobody understood what I was going through.

Just two weeks after Greg's suicide, I flew across the country with my husband to start our lives in San Francisco. I had been thrilled about moving, but now I didn't want to leave the safety and security of my family and friends. As I spoke those words to my family, they pushed me to go, saying, "We'll be fine." They thought I wanted to stay for them; the reality is that I wanted to stay for me. I needed comfort and familiarity. Nonetheless, I got on the plane and cried my way to San Francisco.

Everything changed when we moved. I began working from home, rather than an office. I had no friends and no family nearby, other than my husband, who was struggling to remain connected to me. I was so frightened of meeting people who might ask me typical questions about my family. I was too ashamed to talk about it, but I also didn't want to lie. So I stayed hidden. I became extremely lonely. My family—a pillar of support throughout my life—was shrouded in grief and wasn't emotionally available to help me through this. I isolated myself from old friends. I felt like I had crawled into a hole socially, emotionally, and mentally. There were days I just stayed in my PJs and didn't leave the apartment.

But somehow, someway, I began to heal. It wasn't a moment in time, but a progression of numerous things that began this process.

Thank God for Nancy Kramer and Kelly Mooney, who lead the company I worked for. I credit them for understanding what I did not. They asked Women on Fire's Debbie Phillips, who has worked extensively in grief counseling, to help me. She guided me through the grieving process. Her impact proved to be the catalyst to my recovery. I looked forward to my weekly conversations with her, even though they were the toughest of my life. She gave me permission to be angry, confused, and lonely, to sit with my grief and truly feel it.

I also got very clear about my spiritual beliefs. I had never considered what happened when someone took his or her own life. Because I believe in a caring and healing God, I truly believe that Greg experienced his hell on Earth and is healing in his own Heaven now.

I began looking for signs that he was still with me, and I saw many. After his funeral, we brought home many roses that were on his casket. A single white rose was surrounded by red ones, and the white one continued to flourish the entire time I was at my mom's home. And I felt like it was Greg telling us he was still alive too—maybe more alive than he had been for a long time.

My dreams are full of Greg. Most often, he shows up along-side me in a car, driving by billboards that are snapshots of our memories together. He continually tells me that he's happy and that he is where he needed to be in this lifetime. I miss his physical presence and his hugs, but I am comforted with a recognition that he is still with me.

About nine months after Greg's suicide, life began moving forward. I began working in an office. I put one foot in front of another and attended a couple of social events. My husband surprised me with a trip through Northern California, and then I took him to Seattle. We participated in a 20-mile walk called

"Out of the Darkness," where proceeds went to the American Foundation for Suicide Prevention. We walked the grueling hills of San Francisco through the night and finished to a sunrise service. The symbolism that the sun would shine again was profound and healing. Seeing so many other families walking in support of loved ones opened my eyes to how prevalent suicide is in our country. I didn't feel as alone or isolated after that walk.

THE LESSONS OF GRIEF

And now, almost nine years after Greg's death, I have learned much from this horrific tragedy. I have continued to learn about compassion, acceptance, friendship, love, forgiveness, and more.

I've found the truth in the adage that hindsight is always 20/20. I finally forgave myself, but I held on to guilt for a long time over our not treating Greg's drug problem on a deeper level. We focused, as most families do, on treating the addiction. I realize now that it was a symptom of the problem and not the problem itself. But what was the problem? Mental illness? Sexual abuse? Unfortunately, we will never know because we did not uncover it before it was too late. But if I've learned anything, it is that drugs are used to cover up a bigger problem.

For my own process, I now realize that moving away from familiarity, from family and friends, at the height of my grief made my own healing more difficult. I couldn't separate my grief from the normal feelings that go along with taking on such major life changes.

I isolated myself, but I should have insulated myself. After Greg died, it became easy to shut out the world. Part of this was because of my move, but I also chose not to return calls or emails. I wish I would have chosen a small set of friends I was close to and let them know that I was going to confide in them and keep them close, and that I would need them to keep after me when I began to pull away.

An important lesson was learning that you never know who your biggest supports will be. At first, I was angry for the lack of support I felt from some of those I was closest to. I now know my family was drowning in their own grief, and my husband simply didn't have the tools to help me through this. Thankfully, I had friends who pressed me to talk about my pain, and female mentors in my professional life who had the insight to find extra support for me. Working with a grief counselor gave me the tools and support I needed to finally begin to heal. An appointment each week ensured dedicated time to healing, without any other distractions.

Today, I feel healthier than I've felt in a long time. I am not back to "normal" because I'll never be the same person I was before my brother died. But I've healed and I move forward every day. I am finding my way back to me. I care again. And that is a huge difference. I will always miss my brother, but I've come to understand why he'd want out of his misery, and I forgive him. I feel his presence often. I am comforted and grateful for the precious time he was in my life.

Tricia Simpson, wife to a generous and loving husband, David. Mother to two charming and handsome boys, Grant and Turner. Dublin, Ohio, resident. Perpetual traveler. Serial marketer. Digital branding strategist. Chocaholic. Avid reader. Wannabe marathoner (the half, at least). Wine lover. Spa connoisseur. Co-host of Women on Fire teas in Columbus, Ohio. Seeker of cool stuff for kids to do through Hulafrog. City girl. Nature lover. Planner extraordinaire. Organic mama. Supportive friend to many.

WHAT'S IMPORTANT NOW

*An unexpected caregiver role brings
perspective and strength*

Marilyn Brown

Saturday, February 27, 2010. It started as a fairly typical winter evening. My husband and I were getting ready to go to a campaign event. Eric, Franklin County's probate judge, was running to be chief justice of the Ohio Supreme Court, and the event was with a nice grassroots group in nearby Worthington. We were stopping by to renew our commitment to their work.

I, too, was running for office, in my first re-election bid as Franklin County commissioner. Eric and I both love public service, but running two campaigns simultaneously was very trying, something we never planned to do. Yet, when the current chief justice announced his retirement and Eric was asked to run, he felt the opportunity was not to be taken lightly.

As I was getting dressed, our older daughter, Beryl, called. She was excited; she'd started labor on her third child, and this was the signal for us to be "on call" to take her boys when she and her husband needed to leave for the hospital. Eric and I loved having

Vincent and Max, who were then 5 and 3, in our condominium. I imagined us going to the nearby park and making hot cocoa. Later, Vincent and I would play cards while Max napped.

My phone rang again. This time, it was our other daughter, Daryn, who typically called daily as she walked from work to catch the subway to her Harlem apartment. The calls were chatty, as she is. We were laughing about something, when she suddenly screamed, "MOM, I'VE BEEN HIT BY A CAR!" The words, so out of context, did not register at first.

Her phone must have fallen from her hand, but I could hear a flurry of voices. Someone called out, "Oh no! The girl's been hit. Call the police!" Then there was silence. I was screaming Daryn's name into the phone, but no one responded. Eric dialed Daryn's boyfriend, Ben, who would know the route she was taking. I was sick with fear and frustration, her cries repeated over and over in my head.

A beep on my phone: It was Beryl, texting me that her labor was slowing. I wondered if I should call to tell her of her sister's accident. But what would I say?

Beryl and Daryn are 20 months apart, and so very different. Beryl is an attorney, something she seemed born to do. She's so like her dad, a very smart, analytical thinker. Daryn is more like me, creative and intuitive. From high school, she was interested in theater. After college and internships, she followed her dream to a successful career as a stage manager. On the night of the accident, she had been living in New York City for nine years. Practical Beryl never understood her younger sister's life, nor could she conceive of theater as a viable career for Daryn.

I called Beryl and learned that her labor seemed to have stopped. I told her about her sister's accident. She was devastated, of course, and had so many questions. But we still had no answers.

Finally, we learned that Daryn was taken by ambulance to the closest hospital. Her medical specialist was called because Daryn's health is complicated. She has an orphan (meaning rare) disease called reflex sympathetic dystrophy, also known as complex regional pain syndrome (RSD/CRPS), which began when she was 18. It is a misfiring of the sympathetic and parasympathetic nervous systems that sends pain signals to the brain. The disease began in Daryn's hand after a sprained wrist did not heal well. It spread to both hands and arms. Pain in her muscles and joints are controlled by a medical pump that was installed in her spinal column and abdomen. During the accident, the pump catheter broke; medication leaked out, and her hands clenched closed.

Meanwhile Beryl's labor resumed during the night, and the next morning, we picked up Vincent and Max. The afternoon of Feb. 28, our third grandson, Alex Joseph, was born. Beautiful, smart, wonderful Alex is a special joy to all of us. Sadly, his birth date is forever linked to the accident, a reminder of when Daryn's life circumstances changed.

We learned that while Daryn had not sustained serious injuries from the car hitting her, because of her previous medical condition, she was having other problems. Daryn's catheter was surgically replaced, but soon after her release from the hospital, her legs began exhibiting RSD/CRPS symptoms of burning, crushing pain. There are no good treatments, and certainly no cure for this hideous disease. She and I cried and laughed together through many phone conversations. I didn't know what else to do. I was thankful that she had a supportive boyfriend and other friends, as well wonderful medical care in New York.

A HOUSEHOLD WITH CIVIL SERVANTS

Eric and I have always had campaign staffs that coordinated our work, campaign, and personal calendars. Eric's judicial calendar was more predictable than my county commissioner schedule.

Although commissioners have only two required meetings per week, no two days are ever the same. Between the committee work and boards I chair or serve on, it can be dizzying. Plus, Eric and I constantly had fundraising calls and local and statewide political party events. I was being pulled in many directions, but always I was drawn to go to New York to see Daryn or to spend time with my grandsons.

By mid-2010, our challenges/opportunities changed yet again. The retiring sitting chief justice died suddenly in office, and Gov. Ted Strickland named Eric as his replacement. This meant that Eric had to step down as Franklin County probate judge to be chief justice while running to keep that seat. Our lives were in upheaval. It was exciting and energizing, but it was also an exhausting and frustrating time.

Eric and I met when he was 8 and I was 7. His parents managed a day camp in the Cleveland suburb of Oakwood Village; my mom was the camp secretary. Later, we became camp counselors, but were always only summer friends as we attended rival high schools. He graduated a year ahead of me, and we began dating when he went to college. On my 18th birthday, we became engaged. We were married, in a double ceremony with my sister and her fiancé, the next year. Then, we grew up together. We are best friends, and our relationship continues to grow.

In 2010, we had been married for 37 years, and we had never not been available for one another. Yet, there we were, each of us focused on and consumed by our own campaigns. Eric was gone so much, and I missed my partner.

Then one night, as I was leaving an event, I was threatened at knifepoint by someone asking if I was married to Judge Eric Brown. I quickly jumped into my car, locked the doors and exited the parking area. I called Eric, who encouraged me to stop at the local police department. I refused, saying I was coming home and nothing would stop me. The incident left me an emotional wreck, and I needed to seek counseling. From that point on, I didn't attend any campaign event alone.

I had a bad feeling on election night. We were all at the Hyatt Regency Hotel with the Ohio Democratic Party. Daryn was there, although her medical condition was not great. Eric's family, and my mother, sister, and brother-in-law came from Cleveland. I was nervous about my re-election, and Eric's election was even less certain. As numbers came in, it was clear that everyone on the statewide Democratic ticket was losing, from the governor on down. *But I won my race!* I was extremely proud, but who could I say that to? Nobody wanted to hear it, not even Eric. Our family from Cleveland quickly left to go back home. They saw no sense in staying around after Eric's loss. "Wait a minute," I thought. *"I won!"*

I went up to the hotel room where my daughters were. Daryn was in a lot of pain, and she was upset about her dad losing his race. She and Beryl were hugging each other and crying. What was I to do? This was not the place to be happy for my success. I went to find my campaign staff, and with them I could enjoy a few moments celebrating my victory and accomplishment.

A NEW ROLE AS PROTECTOR

By mid-2011, Daryn realized that, because of her condition, she had to return to Columbus. We supported this decision, and Eric and I prepared our guest room for her.

On December 21, I was in a commissioners' meeting and received a text from Eric asking where to find crutches for Daryn, who had fallen in her room and hurt her foot. I hurried home, and found Daryn with a swollen, purple leg and ankle. We got her to the Ohio State University Emergency Department, where

X-rays showed broken tibia and fibula bones. The orthopedic surgeon decided to insert a rod into her bone.

The surgery went well, and she was home in a couple days with instructions that walking would be good for her. Yet only a day later, her ankle and leg swelled dramatically. Back to the ER and more X-rays. The surgeon was shocked—the rod had shattered through the bone. He operated again to take out the rod and put her in an "external fixator," which looked like scaffolding around her leg, to allow the swelling to go down while they determined the next step. A third surgery fixed the bones with plates and screws. Remember, throughout all this Daryn was still suffering from misfiring signals to her brain, telling it there was unremitting pain. I was horrified at what was happening.

After two weeks at a rehabilitation center, Daryn came home. She began physical therapy and was in a wheelchair for several months. It was challenging for all of us. Our entire condo was taken over with handicap-accessible items. The shower in our master bedroom was the only one Daryn could use, but she needed my help lifting her out of the wheelchair to a shower chair. I'm stronger than the 92 pounds of me look! Thus began a routine. Eric took her to her specialists, physical therapy and her counselor because he had the strength and flexibility to do so. I helped her with showering and other personal care.

For Passover Seder in early April, Beryl and Eric drove to Cleveland to be with family. Daryn had not been feeling well, so I stayed home with her. She was taking a long nap, and late in the afternoon I went to check on her. She was clammy and non-responsive. I strapped her into the wheelchair and took her to the garage. I got her into the car, and she slumped forward. I rushed to OSU Hospital.

A security guard took Daryn in to register while I parked the car. By the time I got inside, I could not find her. Apparently, she had been having difficulty breathing and was immediately taken to a room and hooked up to oxygen. A doctor said she might have congestive heart failure and immediately ordered a heart ultrasound. She was not having trouble breathing when I brought her in. What happened?

No heart problem was found, but her breathing remained compromised for unknown reasons. She was admitted to the intensive care unit, still unaware of what was going on around her. I called Eric, who was just sitting down with his family for Passover dinner. He and Beryl got on the road back to Columbus.

I told myself: "I am here to watch. I am here to protect her from staff who don't know not to stick needles in her right arm because of the RSD/CRPS. I am here to see that blankets and sheets are not put over her hypersensitive legs." I am Daryn's protector. It's an exhausting role, but one I have become super competent and adept at.

Even on the respirator, Daryn wasn't able to breathe adequately. She was moved to a more restrictive ICU room and yet another respirator. There were lots of tests and lots of specialists, but no diagnosis. Daryn remained under constant sedation and pain medication.

When Eric arrived, I fell into his arms. My sanctuary. He and I sat holding hands, all night and all day. Daryn's oxygen levels remained severely low, controlled only by the respirator set on high levels, banging loudly in our ears for several days. A feeding tube kept her fed and hydrated.

I posted updates on Facebook throughout her many treatments and surgeries. I was astonished to received hundreds of comments from Daryn's friends and ours. We received calls and messages from people wanting to help, and visitors stopped by to check on us. Most poignant was Daryn's theater department chair from Ohio Northern University, who saw the post on Facebook. In tears, he told us he needed to see her.

We didn't know what we needed or wanted during the five or six days Daryn was sedated and suffering from what we learned was acute respiratory distress syndrome. The doctors said she was fighting to survive the whole time. And then, in a flash, she awoke as the respirator was being weaned. Her breathing restarted on its own. She is so strong. I'm not sure I could be that strong.

CELEBRATING WHAT MATTERS

Through caring for Daryn, I have learned about perspective and how to balance work and family. This has been a long-time struggle, as I have always maintained a complex schedule. For example, I started graduate school when the girls were in elementary school. Beginning in the mid-1970s, while we lived in the Greater Cleveland area, I began my lifelong work in social justice issues and public service. Over the years, I was involved with women's issues, broke down racially segregated housing patterns in eastern suburbs, and taught and coordinated race relations efforts for Cleveland's business and religious leaders.

When we moved to Columbus in 1992 for Eric to take a position in Attorney General Lee Fisher's office, I became director of Pickerington's Chamber of Commerce, which was a wonderful opportunity for learning about community. Then I moved on to work in a hospice program. This was good for me, as I had admired the work they do. A week before moving to Columbus, my father died of pancreatic cancer. He was in hospice care and died at my parents' home, my home from my birth. Working at a hospice was the most life-affirming work I had ever done.

It is now early 2013. Life has calmed a bit. I have learned so much about myself these past few years. I had long understood what it means to juggle scheduling. Now, I also juggle emotions— frustration, concern, love, care, helplessness—through Daryn's health crises, along with those that come with family life and the demands of my job, including gearing up for a second re-election campaign in 2014, *which I fully intend to win!*

All that I have experienced has changed me. I am not the same person that I was a just few years ago. Daryn has made me a better person. Her ordeals have helped me to see what is important. I am much more engaged and focused on my work. I am motivated to improve the lives of people who need help and are willing to work and be accountable for their actions. I am tougher today. I am more protective of my time and more selective of how, and with whom, I will spend it.

And we may have a new public servant in the family. Beryl plans to run for a seat on her local board of education. I am so proud of her. She follows in the footsteps of her father, Eric, and his father, Carl, who both served as board of education members. Eric first ran in 1977, and Beryl, at 7 months old, was pictured on campaign posters above the quote, "My dad cares about Mayfield Schools, and me too!" Eric was the top vote-getter, and we always thought Beryl's picture did it for him!

Grandsons Vincent and Max, now 8 and 6, are doing great in school. I see definite signs that Vincent is more like his mom and Grandpa Eric. Max has lots of his dad's creativity and is a wonderful student in school. He always listens to his teacher. He is definitely not like his mom and grandpa. Maybe more like me or his Aunt Daryn! Wonderful Alex, the time-marker related to Daryn's accident, is already 3 years old and in preschool class.

Daryn still is in much pain in her feet and legs, often bringing her to the point of tears. Yet, she has come a long way. She walks, most days, without assistive devices. She has specialists, physical therapists, and counselors whom she sees often. She also works out, swims, and walks in our neighborhood. I am very proud of her motivation and hard work.

Eric and I struggle to get time alone, and so now we set up dates. This is very nice. At 39 years of marriage and counting, our bond grows stronger by the day. And with Daryn's improvements, Eric has seen that he can leave her alone at home and go back to working.

My journey has been convoluted. I attended a Women on Fire day-long workshop at the end of 2011 where I said I was not "on fire." Now, I can honestly say, I AM A WOMAN ON FIRE! I am getting things done as never before. I have friends and family around me, supporting me. I am doing what I was meant to do with my life.

Marilyn Brown is a daughter, sister, wife, mother, grandmother, and Franklin County (Ohio) Commissioner, dedicated to social justice and economic sustainability. Her Jewish heritage and teachings of Tikkun Olam, or Repairing The World, are the foundation for her philosophy that economic development, good jobs, and workforce readiness, coupled with a strong safety net, fair elections, diversity and inclusion for all people, and open and accessible access to education, housing, government, and the arts are the cornerstones on which a moral and just society are built. Marilyn and Eric married in 1973 and are still growing up together.

GETTING BACK TO LIFE

Persevering through a mother's catastrophic injuries and illness

Michelle Whittaker

It was a ridiculously cold and windy day, so common for March in Chicago. As native Chicagoans, neither my mom nor I thought anything of the weather as we met at O'Hare Airport, coming in from Memphis and Washington, D.C., respectively. We had a simple plan: do a little shopping on Michigan Avenue before heading over to my grandmother's house where we were staying. I was excited to be spending the week with Mom. Although I loved my life in D.C. working for a congressman, I missed hanging out with her. She was outgoing and friendly, and more and more I modeled my behavior after hers in an attempt to build my new adult life.

We circled the famous shopping district in our compact rental car, searching for a parking spot. After coming up empty, I made the suggestion that will haunt me for the rest of my life: "Let's just pay for parking at Water Tower Place." My mom begrudgingly headed over to the lot, but as we pulled up to the entrance, the neon sign flashed FULL. We continued down Chestnut Street. We were sitting at the traffic light, trying to come up with another parking option. One minute, I was watching people being pushed across the street by the brutal wind, and the next moment I was waking up with huge pieces of metal on top of our car.

The window-washing scaffolding on the 42nd floor of the John Hancock Building had blown off and come crashing down. Attorneys and experts would later learn what had gone wrong mechanically, but at that moment, I knew only that steel had crashed through our car and two other vehicles. People were running around, but I couldn't make sense of their actions.

A man outside the car was telling me to remain calm, that help was on the way. Surprisingly, I did not feel anxious. I started talking to my mom, who I could see was unconscious. "Keep breathing. Help is on the way," I repeated over and over and over. Time seemed to warp, with events happening both quickly and in slow motion at the same time. One second I was inside the car, and the next I was on a stretcher. People were telling me not to look closely at my mom. She would be taken to Northwestern Memorial Hospital, just a few blocks away. I would go to Cook County Hospital. Everything was chaotic, but I knew that I needed to contact my family. My dad was at our family home in Memphis and the least likely to be of immediate help; yet he was the person I most wanted to talk to.

At the hospital, I was examined and given medication for sore muscles, my only injury. My cousin Mike arrived and took me to Northwestern Memorial Hospital, where I found my mother's two sisters in the waiting room. Mom was in surgery, they said, and it would be a while. Dad was aware of the situation and was making arrangements to fly up. Everyone agreed that I needed to go home with Mike to rest. I remember taking two Tylenol with codeine and still feeling the adrenaline of the day flowing through me.

When I was able to see my mom after her 14-hour surgery,

I couldn't stay in the room more than a couple minutes. She was in a coma with all kinds of wires and tubes connected to her. Her arms and legs were propped up in different ways, and she had lost two fingers. The biggest concern, though, was traumatic brain injury. No one knew yet what this would mean.

My dad arrived the next day and gave me the biggest, longest hug of my life. The doctors told him that Mom would never open her eyes again; there was too much brain damage. This news pushed me into an anxiety attack. I felt guilty that I had walked away basically unharmed, while my mother was fighting for her life.

But the next morning we were awakened by a call from the hospital. Mom had opened her eyes and was responding to simple commands, surprising her entire medical team. She would continue to shock them along her road to recovery.

POST-TRAUMATIC STRESS

Eight days after the accident, I returned to D.C. My father felt that I was in over my head emotionally and needed a break. At 23 years old, my carefree life was over. Dad's hope was that my work, which was busy and exciting, could provide distraction. And it did help. My co-workers were kind and inquired about my mother. Then they did the best thing: they returned to normal. Normal was my goal.

My friends outside of work did not follow this playbook. Their concern for my mother's and my well-being was smothering. The constant questions—Is she breathing on her own? Would she be able to walk again? Could she move her hands?—stressed me out. I didn't have clear answers—no one did—and I hated being asked all the time.

I began seeing a therapist, who assured me that these feelings toward my friends were natural. I was diagnosed with post-traumatic stress disorder, and found some comfort in having a label. But I felt isolated. I tried to act as though everything was the same when it wasn't.

Back in Chicago, my mom continued to improve. Once she met specific markers, such as breathing on her own and not needing to be on an IV, she was moved to the Rehabilitation Institute of Chicago, where she began intensive physical, occupational, and speech therapies. Dad rented an apartment nearby.

Around the same time, I moved to Texas and took a position on the campaign of former Dallas Mayor Ron Kirk in his 2002 bid for the U.S. Senate. My job was to oversee that all donations met federal laws. Mayor Kirk often referred to me as the woman who would keep him out of jail. My move was therapeutic as well. I knew that people can sometimes reinvent themselves in a new work environment, and that was perfect for me. Despite my daily calls to Chicago, most of my colleagues had no idea about the accident. I could pretend for a while that it never happened.

As the summer flowed into the fall, Mom regained her ability to speak and was able to use one of her arms. The doctors kept telling my dad that she would not be able to do something, and soon after she would do that very thing.

When the campaign ended in November I was left with no choice but to move in with my parents in Chicago. Mom had been released from the rehab hospital but was going for therapy daily. While my plan was to stay only until I found a new job in D.C., the reality of the situation required that I stay longer. Mom needed 24-hour care and, even with the assistance of a paid caretaker, it was stressful for my dad. So I stayed to help out. My life, like my dad's, was centered on Mom's needs.

One of my friends suggested that I start an online journal as an outlet for my feelings. This turned out to be a godsend, my lifeline to the outside world. My online journal was filled with a recounting of my days, venting about life with my parents, and occasionally daydreams about what I wanted my life to be. I restricted access to my posts to keep the readership small, so it was like a daily conversation with friends. They could not solve the issues I was dealing with, but they were a wonderful sounding board and source of support.

NEW ROLES AND ROUTINES

My parents and I fell into a routine. Dad and I took turns getting ready for the day, and then we got my mom ready together. I would sit with her while she napped after a day of therapy, and Dad would go to the gym or bookstore or just for a walk. It was not an exciting time, but I learned so much about my parents and their relationship.

When I think about my parents, I can't help but think of Clair and Cliff Huxtable from *The Cosby Show*. My parents were both professionals—Dad was an engineer and Mom a high-school guidance counselor—and both had a witty sense of humor. They provided me with a stable, loving home where I always felt supported. I had a special relationship with each of them. My mom and I were shopping addicts. We could spend an entire day at the mall together. Mom also introduced me to theater. It began as a way to get my out of my shell because I was such a shy child, but it became so much more. During high school, Mom and I would attend performances of every touring musical that came through Memphis. We would go to the early service at church, then brunch and a show. Those days were perfect.

Dad and I had a close bond too. When I was young, he would take me fishing. Dad hated reaching into the container of leeches we used for bait, so I did it. As I got older, Dad was always trying to teach me how to fix things on my car or in the house, just in case. I still remember the Saturdays I spent in the garage learning how to change the oil, brake pads, and tires.

I never really thought about them as a couple until the time we spent together in Chicago. It gave me a window inside their relationship. They showed me that you could be with someone but still have a life. Despite the horrible twist of fate, they had nothing but devotion for each other.

As the weeks turned into months, we planned to move Mom back to Memphis. I believed that would mean I could return to D.C. By the time we left Chicago, Mom had shocked all by walking a little bit using a walker. We were ready to create a new reality for ourselves and settle into it.

Then the results of a routine physical upended our plans. Mom was diagnosed with ovarian cancer.

I was sure she would beat it. Why would God allow her to live through such a traumatic accident only to take her away now? She had to beat cancer because that would make the better story. Yet that's not how the tale goes. After battling cancer for nearly a year, my mom passed in July in our home.

EVERYTHING CHANGES AGAIN

On the day Mom died, I had spent the early morning hours beside her. When my dad came in to be with her, I kissed her on the cheek and told her I loved her before heading upstairs for a shower. It was the last time that I saw her alive.

I was working on a puzzle when the hospice nurse came to tell me that Mom was gone. I ran to my parents' bedroom and my dad embraced me, tears streamed down his face. I did not cry. I told Dad I would call family.

Somehow through the first few phone calls, I managed to keep it together. A few tears would fall, but I was under control. After calling my mom's best friend, I felt myself getting weaker. I phoned one of my best friends, Michael. I got his voicemail and left the worst message ever. When I called another close friend, Nilam, I was starting to falter. My dad reappeared, seeming stronger than he had earlier. It felt safe for me to break down.

I opened the floodgates—sadness, anger, confusion, fear, loss. My mom was my best friend. What would I do without her? Who would I turn to? The pain cut to my core. The idea of eating and sleeping seemed ridiculous, although my friends managed to get me to do a little of both over the next few days. The movie *Wimbledon* seemed to be the only thing to calm me down enough to sleep. The DVD remained in my laptop next to my bed.

I did not have to be involved in planning the services. My only task was to help choose clothing for Mom to buried in. I did, but I have no memory of what I selected. I had an anxiety attack before the memorial service in Memphis and did not attend. My dad gave me a Valium, and I had the best night of sleep since Mom passed. I took another one the morning of her funeral in Chicago. That day is cloudy for me. I vaguely remember seeing and speaking to people, but I was numb and in tears.

After the funeral, my dad and I remained at my uncle's house for a few days, or it might have been a few weeks. In my grief, time seemed to stand still. But at some point, I got my "brilliant" idea: I should travel. I am not sure why, but I thought traveling would help me overcome my anguish.

For my first trip, I visited a close college friend in San Francisco. It was August, but it was freezing. Yet the energy of the city distracted me from my pain. We spent days as tourists, then went to Napa Valley. The sun and fresh air brought me a bit of peace. There were still crying spells, but I felt compelled to control them in public. There were two exceptions. One morning I called my dad, who had returned to Memphis, and I learned that he had put our dog, Missy, down. It broke another piece off my heart.

During a visit to a winery, I started chatting with two sisters who had recently lost their mother to a heart attack. The tears flowed as we hugged and shared our grief. These complete strangers understood me in a way my friends could not. I found so much comfort in those moments. When I left San Francisco and headed back to Chicago, I felt as though part of me had healed. What I didn't know was how far I still had to go.

My second travel experience did not go as well. A friend invited me to join her on an extended work trip to London, Johannesburg, and Cape Town. The trip exposed the depths of my sorrow. The first day in London sparked a crying spell while waiting for a train. My pain was so raw that I no longer cared about crying in public. A quick chat with my dad calmed me down, and everyone agreed that it was jet-lag making me more emotional. After a few days, I did feel better.

The flight between London and Johannesburg, South Africa, was 14 hours long. Upon our arrival, those same feelings that led to the tears at the London train station were creeping up on me. A nap seemed like the best move. But it didn't work. Grief flooded my mind. In an attempt to get a grip, I went on a tour of Johannesburg and Pretoria the next day. It was not exactly uplifting. The tour group consisted only of me and two Polish couples who spoke little English, and on view during the trip was the most extreme separation between the haves and the have-nots I had ever experienced.

By the end of the day, I was so sad and anxious that all I could think about was how to get home. There was no reasoning with me. I didn't care about the plans we had made for Cape Town or that my friend would be joining me for sightseeing. I booked myself on an Air France flight for the next day.

My journey home was not an easy one. I was so tired that I fell asleep almost immediately after getting settled on the plane. I woke up two hours later to discover that we had not moved an inch. There were mechanical problems, and they were not sure they could be repaired with the available parts. Another few hours passed before they told us that we would not be leaving that day. Unfortunately, the conference my friend was attending was so large that all hotels were full. I was too ashamed to return to the room with my friend, so I spent the night in the Johannesburg Airport, sleeping between two chairs in the lounge of KLM Airlines. The flight finally took off the next afternoon, but the timing was off. When we landed in Paris, we had missed the connecting flights, causing more delays. I was exhausted and frazzled by the time I finally made it home.

STEPPING BACK INTO MY LIFE

Back in Memphis, I still felt lost. I had no idea who I was or what I wanted to do. My friends had been living their lives and working, while my life had stood still for three years. I didn't know how to jump back in or what my next steps should be. My dad encouraged me to wait until the lawsuit from the accident was resolved so I would have a better understanding of my choices.

I struggled through the fall. My crying spells would get shorter for a few weeks, and then something would happen, and I would find myself in bed for days. Things got better when I enrolled in a couple of classes at the local university. I began to feel stronger. The lawsuit was finally settled, and it provided me with opportunities for change. It was time to leave Memphis.

I decided to move back to the D.C. area I loved. I purchased a condo in Arlington and began to renovate it. But, although I reconnected with old friends and made some new ones, when I wasn't forced to go out, I preferred to stay home alone. Without my realizing it, grief had turned me into a hermit.

The road to full recovery involved therapy and some of the most patient friends on earth. It has been scary reconnecting with the woman I was before the accident and making her a part of the woman I am today. Each day I wake up and try to start the day with a grateful heart. Through everything, I know that I am here for a reason. Some days I am here to be a good, supportive friend. Other days, I am here to be a reminder of my mother's legacy. I still wish that I could define my purpose more clearly, but life is not that simple. I am happy if I can live a life that would make my mother proud.

When not exploring the far corners of the world, **Michelle Whittaker** can be found in Washington, D.C. with her 6-year-old miniature schnauzer that dictates her travel schedule. As an active member of the D.C. area knitting community, Michelle often hangs out in yarn shops and coffee shops knitting with friends. Last summer she took the plunge into writing her first play, *The Hair Chronicles*, with graduate school friends. Michelle also enjoys going to the theater, visiting Virginia wineries and absorbing pop culture in all forms.

LEANING INTO GRIEF

Feeling my way toward healing

Lisa Umberger Arundale

Grief

Grief, you wash over me like the ocean waves
*   break across a sandy beach,*
disrupting the shell of calm I have created.
I pensively court the knowing that you will pounce upon
me
again and again, stirring my soul with each visit,
rendering me helpless against my sorrow,
forcing me to take an inventory and build the shell again
with whatever you have left me.

Grief, I fear you are here to destroy me, Until…
after many visits, I realize the sands that make up my soul
are still with me, you have not taken them.
They are merely rearranged.

> *Grief, now I see that when you go, you leave*
> *   behind precious gems,*
> *shooting beams of Light from deep within.*
> *That is what I have felt bumping, breaking my shell.*
> *I once thought it protected me from your harm,*
> *but instead, it held me separate from your gifts.*
>
> *Grief, always your visit leaves me with that which*
> *I would not have known if you had not come.*
> *I have only to let go, and all things are revealed,*
> *for the heart that is breaking, is but opening again.*

In a few days, it will be a year since my husband passed away. On one hand, I cannot believe it has been 11 months and 12 days since I last saw his face, watched his eyes light up when I entered the room, or felt his touch. The loss is still raw. On the other hand, each day has seemed like an eternity, some even longer. Time has simultaneously passed as quick as lightning and as slow as molasses.

Intellectually, we can understand the dynamics of grief, the part it plays in our lives, but it shows up so differently in every person that it is impossible to actually prepare for it. I was not a stranger to loss or grief when I met Dwight. I wrote the above poem in 1997, about six months after my mother was killed in a head-on collision. While my family and I were very close and my previous losses were deeply painful, nothing prepared me for the loss of my husband, my partner, my constant companion. It seeped into the smallest openings of my being and is still molding a new me.

Dwight and I met, ironically, in hospice. I was there to sing for his wife, who I had met a year into her terminal diagnosis. Who could ever have imagined that the man I met that day would become my friend and, later, my husband? Dwight was known for living every moment to the fullest. One lifelong friend described him as her "Peter Pan." He was a fighter pilot, savvy entrepreneur, "celebrating artist" (as he jokingly described himself) and someone who never stopped learning. We didn't date; we just came together. Our relationship started in the middle, with no beginning. Whether traveling the world or staying at home, we were together 24/7.

I learned how to love myself more by experiencing how much he loved me. He didn't believe in Valentine's Day because each day was Valentine's Day to him. We showed our love for each other every day. It wasn't contrived; it was effortless. I had been a "yeller" before Dwight, but he taught me to talk out a disagreement calmly and lovingly. During our first argument, he looked at me with a wry smile on his face and asked, "Why are you yelling? I'm standing right in front of you." I started laughing and learned a whole new way to express myself, even when upset. We made ourselves vulnerable to each other and opened our hearts fully, a gift I will carry forward forever.

Who would have imagined that two years after we met, he too would be diagnosed, go through agonizing, aggressive chemotherapy and radiation, only to have the disease return two years later? Or that the next year I would say goodbye to him where we had first met, in hospice?

Perhaps his diagnosis of cancer in the second year of our relationship created an environment in which we grew closer than we might have otherwise. Or perhaps because he had lost a wife to cancer, he realized that life is fragile and sometimes short. Or maybe we were simply madly in love. I don't know why were we able to have this most amazing life together in only five years, I only know that we did. During our time together, I learned more from him about love, gratitude, and living life to the fullest than I had learned in the preceding 50 years of my life.

A FOG DESCENDS

I remember few details about the days after he died—one of the blessings of grief is that, as time passes, some of the hardest parts disappear from our memories. I was numb in those early moments, and very happy for it. I do remember the desperate need I had to sit in his favorite chair, touch what he might have touched, hold his phone, put my hands on the door handles, anything I thought might still have a part of him lingering on it. I held his clothes and breathed in his scent. I wrapped myself in the sheets he had slept on. I laid my head on his pillowcase. I wore his shirts.

Confusion, forgetfulness, exhaustion, and a feeling of overwhelm became constant companions. I've always believed in a higher power, and this experience both deepened my belief and challenged it. I was aware that the world was going on around me, but I couldn't quite understand how to be in it. If you've ever fainted, there's a moment when the things around you take on a slow-motion, fuzzy effect. You know something is happening to you, but you can't quite understand it or do anything to stop it. I lived in this type of fog for months after Dwight's death. Much later, when a few of the layers of the mist had lifted, I realized how important it had been to my healing. Without the fog, the pain would have been impossible to bear.

Grief didn't just affect my mental and emotional states; it also played out in my physical life. I broke my thumb, tripped over a gas pump, fell off a barstool, and had a myriad of aches, pains, and bruises. Things that my body used to maneuver easily and automatically just didn't compute in my brain. I realized at one point that I hadn't brushed my teeth for, well, an embarrassingly long period of time. It just never crossed my mind.

In the days right after Dwight passed away, it was comforting for my best friend Suzi to stay with me. It was also important for her to return to her home and leave me to get used to living alone again. My staying in our home, the house Dwight and I had shared, instead of selling it right away, felt safe, warm, and like a big hug from Dwight. Sometimes I would go into the room where he last rested and sit in the quiet. I would talk to him. TUG, our puppy—named for a word Dwight had coined and we said every day of our lives: It stands for "Thank U God"—always becomes calm when he enters this room. He was with us the night that Dwight passed away and signaled Dwight's last breath with three barks, the first time he had barked in days.

I found solace in going through Dwight's things by myself a little at a time. The first time I laughed after his death was when I cleaned out a section of his closet and moved over some of my things. He had always teased me about encroaching on his side of the closet, so after I hung my jackets in the space where his shirts once hung, I said out loud to him, "See what happens when you leave me? I take over your closet." I laughed, and then I cried.

RE-ENTRY INTO SOCIAL LIFE

There was no shortage of "helpful" advice, but I found one piece absolutely maddening: "Don't make any big decisions the first year." It sounds perfectly sensible and I would agree, except that there are huge decisions that have to be made during that first year: taxes—both estate and personal—family issues, jobs, possible changes in domicile, distribution of property. I needed help just doing simple things like paying bills and filing. Hiring someone to help me reduced my stress level greatly.

I was both honored to have and sometimes felt burdened by advice from well-meaning friends: "Dwight loved you and he would want you to go out with friends, move on with your life, to sing again." Most of the time I barely had enough energy to get out of bed, so instead of feeling encouraged, I often felt more pressure because I was afraid I was letting my husband down.

Everything someone said to me was magnified in my heart. I felt things at a level I had never felt before. That's saying a lot, as I have been told my whole life that I am "too sensitive." I found that even people who were well meaning often said and did the most bizarre things when they encountered me. Unfortunately, I also learned that some people could be outright cold and hurtful.

About five weeks after Dwight's death, I ventured out with my step daughter-in-law to our small, local grocery store. A stranger asked her why I was crying when a friend hugged me. When told that my husband had died, she turned to me and announced loudly, "Oh honey, you are young and beautiful. Don't you worry; you'll find another man in no time!" She seemed shocked when I burst into loud sobs. She walked off mumbling that she was only trying to help.

A few months later, I decided to go to a friend's birthday party. Parties or large gatherings were overwhelming for me, but I felt comfortable going to this one because I knew the friends well and could escape easily if I needed to. I planned to stay just long enough to say happy birthday, but not long enough for anyone to engage me in a discussion about my husband. I made one miscalculation—wine. By the time I arrived, most guests were on their second or third glass. I was greeted head on with a sloppy hug and, "Oh, the last time I saw Dwight was when he won two dollars off me playing golf. He was a great guy. I just don't understand how he could be so healthy and then…" The man went on and on before realizing I had turned away in tears. He was amazed that his reminiscing hadn't been a comfort to me.

But the most difficult situation by far was a dinner where I was part of a fivesome in an unfamiliar city. Being a fifth wheel was something I was not ready for, as I didn't know there was to be a second couple. When I realized there would be five of us for dinner, it took all the strength I had not to bolt to the elevator and back to the safety of my hotel room. The evening culminated in a huge drama around paying the check. When it arrived, a poor attempt at a joke by one of the men made an already uncomfortable evening for me one of humiliation and pain. I sat stunned as I heard these words: "Lisa's a wealthy widow now, she can pick up the check." Hearing myself referred to as a widow for the first time, and so insensitively, was one of the most hurtful things I endured this past year.

On the way back to the hotel, I was relegated to the middle of the backseat. Riding along, trying to keep myself balanced, I realized I was inside a metaphor for my own life. I felt out of control and definitely was not in the driver's seat. I made the decision that I would become my own best friend and begin to fervently guard myself from situations like this one. And I have. I care much less about what others think of me now. "This is who I am and this is where I stand" became my mantra for dealing with the world.

I became more proficient at excusing myself, walking across the room to get away from anything making me feel uncomfortable, or just leaving if I began to feel drained of energy. I learned to be good to myself, but hopefully still gracious to those who were merely trying to help. There is truth to the saying "humor is tragedy plus time." It has taken months for me to find these situations humorous, but I heard myself laughing about this last story when I recently shared it in my grief group.

I was asked out a month ago and eventually went on a date. The friendship that developed showed me that, as much as I love Dwight, there is room inside me to allow love again. It did amazing things for my self-esteem to know that someone else could find me attractive and interesting.

Before he arrived, I stood in front of my mirror, fondling the ring I had never taken off since our wedding ceremony. I asked Dwight what to do. Before I knew it, the ring was in my right hand. I do not remember the motion of taking it off, but there it was. In my heart, I knew that Dwight wanted me to be happy and to experience love again. I now wear the ring around my neck on a gold chain that was Dwight's.

My year included a trip to Paris with Women on Fire that introduced me to 10 amazing women who have become my rock this year. I could not have imagined getting through this trauma without having depended on these amazing women. When I needed to reach out to someone I could trust they would hear me, love me, and allow me to dig into my feelings without judgment.

AHA MOMENTS

Somewhere along the way, as I realized how deeply grief was touching me. I, perhaps as a result of the years I was a corporate training specialist, made a decision not to let the potential learning that I could get from this experience escape me. So I began journaling my "aha" moments and discoveries. These tips are from my notes:

- I learned that I did not grieve in the same way other people grieved, and that there is NO right or wrong way as long as I was being true to my feelings. I tried to allow whatever came up for me to be the thing that I handled in that moment. I had to concentrate on one thing at a time or the feeling of being overwhelmed would take over very quickly. I could easily sink into a mound of tears, fears, and cascading emotions, and often did during the first few months.
- I also learned to say no without guilt. I found out the hard way not to make long-term commitments, especially those where I was expected to be somewhere every week at a specific time. The person I once had been wanted to take on projects, but the person I was now, inside thick fog, couldn't handle it and I would end up canceling. I even gave myself permission to say no after I had first said yes.

- Crying often and deeply was cathartic. I always felt lighter and better able to handle things after I had a good cry.
- It helped me to write emails rather than talk on the phone. I felt I was able to think about what I wanted to say more clearly. But I also kept a list of friends and their phone numbers next to the phone. When I was sinking into pain, I could reach out to one of them easily and effortlessly.
- It was easier for me to fall asleep on the sofa and then go to bed without fully waking up. Somehow, I didn't feel as alone falling asleep in a chair instead of in a huge, empty bed.

Perhaps the biggest gift I received from Dwight and this experience of loss is a better understanding of love itself. Prior to meeting Dwight, I had associated love with hurt, eventual disappointment and control, with a few nice gestures thrown in between. Dwight taught me that love is always present, always in the forefront, always the guide everything in life is filtered through. Love is the way to approach anything and everything. Love is present in anger, in hurt, and in argument. Love is present in friendship, in business, and in play. Love is gratitude and thoughtfulness. Love is not just the destination; it's the path to getting wherever we are looking to go. Love does not belong to just one person; it is shared between all. It can't be used up; it expands and grows. The more we love, the more we can love. As the song goes: "And love in your heart wasn't put there to stay / Love isn't love... 'til you give it away."

In loving myself enough to allow the pain of loss to take me wherever it wanted, I have gained a new capacity for loving and being loved. Dwight will always be my love, and if I meet another amazing man, there will be plenty of room for Dwight and for anyone that this new man has loved as well. I didn't understand that until I opened my heart to both love and pain.

Don't be afraid of grieving. Let it consume you and turn you inside out, for it is rebuilding you. Without it, you could never become all you can be. In order to build a new house, the builder sometimes has to tear down the old one.

Lisa Umberger Arundale was born and raised in the Appalachian Mountains of Virginia. She composed and performed songs for Virginia's governor, lieutenant governor, attorney general, U.S. congressman and senator, as well as President Gerald R. Ford. As owner of The EnterTRainment Company, she combined her musical and training skills as a corporate consultant for Boeing, Microsoft, Riddell, Eli Lilly and many others. Her audiences have included Elizabeth Taylor, Clint Eastwood, Robert Guillaume and Wayne Dyer. She has performed in Canada, the Philippines, Africa, Italy and Turkey. Lisa has several CDs to her credit and lives in southwest Florida and Martha's Vineyard.

FINDING MY NEXT

How I decided what to do with the third third of my life

Jan Allen

Mostly, I hear with my ears.

But a handful of times over my life someone has said something that has landed throughout my whole body—a shudder, a twinge, a feeling of having been physically touched or hit—and my world shifted.

This was one of those times.

My precious 4-year-old friend Vivian, her mom, Amy, and I were playing "lemonade stand" when Vivi told me she was going to marry her classmate Henry. Excited, I shared that I couldn't wait to attend her wedding. But she stopped me in my tracks when she looked up and said, "No, you'll probably be in heaven." I averted my eyes so she couldn't see my tears, feeling deep in my gut (not my head) that something so important could happen and I just wouldn't be here for it. I was 60; she was 4. She could be right.

It strikes each of us differently, at the oddest times, this deep, visceral feeling that our time left to live is now definitely shorter than the time we've already lived. For some, it is precipitated by a changed face, wrinkled, a little slack, in the mirror. For others, it's a time of transition out of a lengthy career or full-time work, or being among a group of colleagues—young and talented and likely better at technology than you—who have no idea of your earlier contributions, at one time so revered. They weren't around when you made them. This is something I experienced from both sides: I went from being the youngest person on a governor's senior team my first time in public service to the oldest, except for the governor himself, the second time around. I realized I was the same age as the senior "gray hair" we thought of as the old guy during my first stint there.

For still others, it's the realization that there is probably time for one or two more dogs, or one more refrigerator.

It's the stark moment when we more fully *feel*, in a way that we had not felt it before, one of the central sorrows of life: we grow old and die.

A TIME OF DESPAIR

I had that moment after Vivian's biting observation. I fell into despair, depressed for months. Here was a problem I couldn't merely think my way through or rehearse and experiment with over and over until I got it right. Added to this gloom was harsh self-judgment. My life has been wonderful, full of blessings and good work. Why couldn't I just be grateful? Every door that has opened in the past has meant a little sorrow or nostalgia at what was being left behind, but it was always outweighed by the promise of what lay ahead. For the first time ever, I wondered—as I entered this new phase of life—could opening this door mean more sorrow and less promise?

Then, to top it off, I heard what some Harvard undergrads said when they were asked what came to mind when they thought of someone 60 or older. They responded with wrinkled, washed up, useless. Which couldn't have been farther from the way I felt.

I've had a lifelong habit of going deeper and examining life at many levels, and I'd been arrogant enough to think I had this personal development thing licked. Rocked and disoriented, I started to wonder: What was this disconnect between how I was feeling and what the world was saying about people my age? Was it just me or was something more happening here?

It turns out that something was, and is, happening, and it's big. Our eulogies for 60-year-olds have gone in one generation from "she lived such a long fulfilling life" to "she died so young." We're living much longer. We have extra years, after midlife but before decline and death—a new third third of life, from 60 to 90, and maybe beyond.

How we are aging is changing too. Most of us think of aging as a time of steady decline after health peaks in midlife. But more and more people are staying healthy, or relatively so, well into their 90s, right up to the last day, or week or month, because we now know that much of what we consider "aging" is really the result of sedentary living.

As has happened many times, what truly woke me up to this new reality was a role model of mine, a woman in her mid-80s, someone ahead of me on the path who has broken through the stereotypes about the third third of life. She's engaged in full-time work, including completing a two-year national effort at 83 or 84 that kept her on the road and in important decision-making rooms. She is still putting up Christmas lights on the outside of her house by herself (heck, I've never done that!), and she looks beautiful in a chic suit and high heels on New Year's Eve.

Wait a minute! We have choices? Even in this life stage?

NOW WHAT?

Surprised that I was surprised by that—but energized by the realization that I may have 25 or 30 or even 40 years left, which are mine to make the best of—I began to dig into a particular paradigm that seemed to have me frozen in place and was causing such despair. It is a paradigm called *retirement*, something that most of us spend a lifetime working toward because, after all, isn't it the promised land? I found some dirty little secrets surrounding retirement.

The concept of retirement was made up by the leisure industry about 50 years ago as a time of play and self-focus, a linear model that some characterize as Learn, Work, Rest, Die. This may look good to you when you're 40, juggling career and family, gasping for air and more time. But people who have arrived at this life stage confess their private distress to me all the time, asking, "Now what?" They often feel bored, restless, irrelevant, or dismissed.

Why? Because we might be built to play for a handful of years, but not 30 or 35. As human beings, we need some structure to stay motivated and relevance to something or someone beyond ourselves to be happy.

As I reached out to share and talk to my contemporaries, I found that I was not alone. For many, entering this life stage induces a second identity crisis. We all experienced this search for identity earlier in life, but this time brings a new and unsettling twist. Aging is a time of not just development, but of development with a heightened sense of mortality. It takes a new kind of courage and resolve to face up to it. As adolescents, we at least felt as though we had a long time to get it right. In the third third, the stakes are at their highest.

There are also challenges around intimacy: Our children grow up and maybe move away; social networks can dwindle if we leave the workplace; friends move to other climates or begin to die. Losses—of people, bodily functions, opportunities—and the gut-level knowledge that someday we are going to have to say goodbye to everyone can overwhelm.

Whew! How, I wondered, do I begin to think about and approach *this* challenge?

FACING THE THIRD THIRD

For me, it meant going back to the two bedrock principles that guide my life. The first, from the great psychoanalyst and thinker Vicktor Frankl, is that happiness is the byproduct of a meaningful life. Meaning comes from what we give to the world, what we experience in the world (love, art, nature, beauty), and courage in the face of suffering. The second principle is that all of life is a choice between growth and decay, between deep change and slow death. The minute something is born, it begins to die—unless we intervene to keep it growing.

I realized that I needed to continue to grow beyond myself, in ways that provided meaning and connection, to prevent the many losses in this life stage from overwhelming me. What became clear to me is that the real threat to vital living in the leisure industry's concept of retirement is that we see it as a *destination*, a place to *stop*, not a place to continue to grow. But *stopping* is the way of decay, of slow death.

Fortunately, many big thinkers are proposing new paths—encore careers, a portfolio life, intentional communities, lifelong learning. All are good ideas, but as a smart friend said to me while discussing these choices, "I don't want one more standard to live up to or only one way to live this life stage. That's what we have now. *I want choices.*"

Then it dawned on me: Rather than *one* answer, what we

really need is a guiding question to reach into this rich complexity and take us beyond a one-way-only path.

What if we retire retirement as the only choice and replace this so-called destination with a continuing journey and a guiding question to propel ourselves forward through this new life stage? What if each of us committed to asking, from this day until our last, "What is my Next?"

I see people doing just that. One friend is cutting back on her day job to indulge a real passion: helping people rear healthy dogs and, by so doing, become more healthy themselves. Another is very actively serving on the board of an organization she once led. And my mother, who goes to an adult activities center and has found new ways to feel a sense of purpose, is helping prepare boxes for veterans, welcoming the newcomers. But these changes came only after, in the ever-increasing quiet that comes from her descent into Alzheimer's, she looked up one day and expressed the first feeling we'd heard in two years: "I feel useless." We asked the question for her: What is your Next?

I see others struggling, not recognizing that to live this life stage vibrantly means becoming the CEO of Me Inc., not in a sense of being self-interested but of recognizing that now, more than ever, we are in charge of guiding our own lives. I've heard many people say, "This is the first time I've ever had to really think about it." In our youth and middle age, cultural expectations and support, career and life trajectories with clear roles pulled us forward, but none of those things is on our side now.

Now, the phone may not ring as often or our defining titles might be a thing of the past. We're told to begin to move on, as a very successful lawyer friend of mine was recently admonished, even though she has grown a new practice area and new clients for her firm over the last five years. Now it's up to us to find our own meaning, enlarge our circle of friends, spur our own growth.

LIVING WITH INTENTION

Growth. Purpose. Connection. These are things that keep us vibrant at every life stage. The people my age whom I see thriving are those who have learned to intentionally put these three things into their lives. I take this from them: It's *my* job to create a life of continued expansion, guided by my bedrock principles.

My design may look different from anyone else's—that's part of the beauty of this life stage. When we're somewhat freed from striving for success, we can focus more on meaning. When the kids are grown, we can think more broadly about what we may want to leave for future generations. With the ability to use our skills, knowledge, and experience to think up novel solutions to problems—a characteristic of our brains at this age called *crystallized intelligence*—we can have more impact, often with less time and effort.

We can each choose our pace and sense of balance—how much work, how much play, how much time spent with family and friends. The possibilities are infinite, but at least for me, I have had to put on my big-girl pants to take advantage of them. I was spurred on when a wise young friend said to me—while I was wallowing in my sadness about being in the third third of life—"Gosh, Jan, how tragic it would be to waste this gift of extra time because you didn't keep motivating yourself to fully live it."

So, in addition to my regular coaching practice, coaching leaders and emerging leaders of all ages, I've launched a new social enterprise called 3rd/3rd Ignited (www.3rd3rdignited.com.) to help others navigate this territory and to connect them to resources to make their "Next" happen, whatever that might be for them.

It is helping me induce my own growth as a thinker, a speaker, a blogger, a workshop leader, and a coach. I must consistently learn new skills, refine my point of view, develop new tools. It has given me a deep sense of meaning, a way to be in the lives of others that will help them. And it is deepening my connections to old friends and bringing many, many new people into my life. At any given moment, when my anticipatory grief threatens to overwhelm me, I can take a deep breath and remind myself to focus on what I can give and how I can engage now.

Is it easy? Nope.

First, my discernment process to answer the question about my Next was long. All I knew was that things didn't feel right, that I didn't feel drawn forward. Honestly, I feared never being interested in anything again. So I put my coaching skills into service to myself and started paying attention to and noting any little thing that gave me energy. What was I drawn to read? Where did I feel a tug or pull?

Second, I drew on what I had learned about transitions from the author William Bridges, who said that transitions begin with an ending, then proceed through a neutral zone (although I would call it a "way upset and sometimes very depressed zone") and on to a new beginning. I gave myself permission to be in that neutral zone—what my BFF Debbie Phillips and I call "the mucky middle"—without self-judgment and without telling myself stories that would make it an even ickier time. It is through the stories we tell ourselves that we suffer. During the worst moments, I reminded myself that I would move through this transition if I would only allow the process to unfold.

Third, I finally began to discern my Next out of all the little nigglings I had been noting over time, even though I had no clue how to move forward. I had to create what I needed and wanted, but there was no road map. There are still days when I don't have any idea what I'm doing. But I take a step, and a next step and a next, deeply believing that these little steps will add up to something useful.

Fourth, I know that I can't do it alone. So I began to throw my people up around me, gathering 20 people together for a session around concepts and language.

I auditioned to do a TEDx talk on this subject. I did it to create a gap, something to work toward, something that would help refine my thinking. I wanted the rigor of someone else's process to propel me forward. Once I was selected to give a talk, I relied heavily on two friends to react to and offer suggestions on every draft. I created my own team of helpers: one person was good at Web stuff, another one at thinking, and a third energized me by believing in me and providing feedback.

I've been a problem-solver all my life, making lemons into lemonade and even amping it up from time to time with a shot of this or that. But I've realized I'm not going to "solve" this one. I cannot avoid dying. But here is what I CAN do: *I can make darned sure that I do not die before I'm dead.* I can do this whenever I feel less than fully alive by surveying the endless number of possible paths still before me, and asking—and answering—the gentle question: "What is my Next?"

A lawyer, social worker, public relations professional, and veteran of government and politics, **Jan Allen** has synthesized her skills as strategist, businessperson, and change agent to coach leaders and emerging leaders. Visit www.janallen.org. In addition to serving in executive roles for two governors of the state of Ohio, Jan created and led successful public affairs and public relations businesses before beginning her coaching practice. In her latest endeavor as the founder of 3rd/3rd Ignited (www.3rd3rdignited.com), Jan provides maps and apps to help those in the third third of life to live vibrantly. She is also a senior adviser to Women on Fire.

PHOTO: ROB BERKLEY

Standing: Heike Vogel, Maria Verroye, Sophfronia Scott, Lisa Umberger Arundale, Linda Neff, Kacy Cook, Kim Davis, Beth Bryce, Laurel Hodory, Jenifer Madson, Kay Raypholtz, Carrie Saba, Sarah Elizabeth Greer, Michelle Whittaker, and Meredith Schoenberger. *Sitting:* Mary Kay Purdy, Susan Kruger, Marilyn Brown, Debbie Phillips, Tricia Simpson, Leah Hamilton, and Marge Snyder. Missing from the photo are Mary Carran Webster, Nicole Friedler Brisson, and Jan Allen.

ACKNOWLEDGMENTS

It takes a village to produce a book, and I am deeply grateful for the creative forces and dedication of every single person who added her or his magic to this one.

This is the second book in our Women on Fire series—and the first book from our new publishing company, Women on Fire Media.

My whole-hearted appreciation starts with the readers and supporters of our first, award-winning book; they inspired this second volume. Your cards, letters, and emails—in addition to our in-person meetings at many events and book signings—reinforced in my bones how essential it is to tell stories of real-life women triumphing over their struggles. Thousands of women saw themselves in those stories, and then they could imagine a way forward in their own lives. So, of course, Volume 2, featuring more stories of hope and inspiration, had to be born!

For it, I engaged the talented writer and experienced publisher Sophfronia Scott to spearhead the project as publisher. Packed inside a kind and gentle exterior, Sophfronia is a powerhouse. And I am grateful for her devotion to writing, her many resources and connections, and her friendship and guidance in all aspects of this book.

Author Kacy Cook returned as editor to help the co-authors powerfully craft their chapters. Kacy and I met as 20-year-old editorial clerks at *The Columbus* (Ohio) *Dispatch* and *The Citizen-Journal*. My deep respect for her, then and now, knows no bounds. Her reverent care and joyful enthusiasm for each co-author's story was extraordinary.

Sophfronia, Kacy, and I treasure and thank the 21 co-authors who shared their hearts and souls to create this book. For most of them, it is the first time they are publicly revealing an event, circumstance, secret, or struggle that shaped their lives. It is enormously courageous to reveal one's self to the world, and each and every co-author did so in order to serve others. Thank you, precious and powerful women. Enjoy what is to come and know that your stories will touch many people.

Our team at Women on Fire is the best! Since 2003, I have been fortunate to work with many talented women and men. I can never thank you all enough.

Designer Sebastian Kaupert has guided with sophistication and fun the way Women on Fire is visually presented. He created our logo, the beautiful book cover, and the inside pages. Headshot genius Peter Hurley took the cover photo.

Meredith Schoenberger has brought dynamic and fresh perspective to our team. She provided insightful comments on the book and videos and is in charge of communications and book promotion.

Dianne Phillips is our member care director extraordinaire. Daren Stinson orchestrates the smooth operation of our office. Costas Peppas advises on technology and infrastructure. Amber Miller and Peggy Champlin are our web assistants.

I have unending gratitude for Regina Blos, our resident angel.

Filmmaker Maria Giacchino joined our team for this project and, along with Sophfronia Scott, interviewed 18 of the 21 co-authors. She created powerfully dazzling videos to accompany this book and was pure joy to work with.

Thank you to literary agent Steve Troha for help in selecting the cover and your publishing wisdom. Coffee with you makes any day a holiday! Ditto for best-selling author RoseMarie Terenzio, whose big heart and hand of support are always at the ready.

Love to you Agapi Stassinopoulos for inspiring the first of our now-famous teas and for your generous and exuberant support of this book.

Best-selling author and speaker Marianne Williamson has long been an important teacher and touchstone in my life. We first met when I traveled with her to Bali in 1999. Your "you go, girl!" means the world to me, Marianne.

Great thanks to our superb audio producers Jimmy Parr of Parr Audio on Martha's Vineyard and Dave Elliott of VoxNow in Naples, Florida.

Over the years, many terrific photographers have captured the joy of Women on Fire events. Thank you to Heather Stone, Jinsey Dauk, Peter Hurley, Shannon McCaffery, Nancy Lambert, Josephine Donatelli, Jamie Eslinger, Renata Ramsini, and Rob Berkley.

For years there has been a steady stream of supporters cheering on the mission of Women on Fire to provide inspiration, strategies, and support for women to live lives of their dreams. We feel your love:

Becky Adams, Janette Barber, Edward Beck, Judy Blume, Kelly Boggs, Barry Brown, Bob Campana, Bobbie Celeste, Christopher Celeste, Elle Celeste, Julia Celeste, Noelle Celeste, Terri Cole, Debbie Cook, Betsy Dee, Trudy Dujardin, Jill Dulitsky, Anne Gallagher, Ann Graham, Stedman Graham, Rosanne Halcik, Susan and Joe Henson, Drs. Tom and Cheryl Hoffman, Angela Ittu, Robert Joerger, Nancy Kramer, Catherine Law, Claudia Miller, Daniel Granholm Mulhern, Tandi Musuraca, Emily Neal, Nancy Neal, Jan Nolte, Scott Phillips, Pam Putney, Beth Rose, Mary Jo Ruggieri, Janina Sebesky, Barbara Sher, Curt Steiner,

Rachel Stukey, Trudy Taylor, Loung Ung, Anna Viragh, Marika Viragh, Ellen Wingard, and Michele Woodward.

Jan Allen, my best friend for 30 years, is a co-author in this volume. She is an invaluable resource and support for me and our entire Women on Fire community.

Heaps of appreciation also go to the fabulous co-authors from our first book: Ginny Barney, Allison Barry, Kelley Black, Patricia Wynn Brown, Kacy Cook, Andrea Dowding, Laurie Forster, Lori Phillips Gagnon, Holly Getty, Natalie Griffin, Susan Glavin, Robin Hughes Ingles, Vicki Irvin, Mary Ellen Jones, Shannon McCaffery, Debra Taylor, Theresa Volkmann, and Regina Weichert. Our beloved Jacqueline Pimentel died shortly after publication. Her story of turning 50 and going to Harvard has been a gift that has lived on and inspired many women to return to college.

We love to pieces and thank our Women on Fire members and the weekly readers of the Spark!

The staff at Lady Mendl's Tea Parlour in New York City, the home of Women on Fire teas, remains steadfastly our heroes. Thank you Shawn, Catherine, Scott, Alberto, and your entire team.

I will never stop thanking filmmaker Kathleen Laughlin and playwright Irene O'Garden for inspiring our Women on Fire name. They sparked my imagination when I was only a woman with a dream.

To my engaging mother, Mary Lue Phillips, Women on Fire member #000001 and the greatest influence for my work. You showed me a key to success and happiness in a women's life is someone to believe in her and cheer her on. That made all the difference in my life.

And last, Women on Fire exists because of the love, patience, brilliance, and encouragement of my partner in work and life, my husband Rob Berkley. You are the very epitome of a Man on Fire!

The gratitude expressed here is mostly mine. So you can

imagine with 21 co-authors the appreciation is multiplied substantially to all who supported their efforts as well.

I thought it took a village, but now I realize it's a city of support that brought this book into existence. Thank you all!

20 ASPIRATIONS OF WOMEN ON FIRE

Are you a Woman on Fire? Ask yourself the following.

Do I:

- Desire deep fulfillment in my work and life?

- Cheer on the successes of other women?

- Embrace my talents and achievements?

- Eagerly share my information, ideas, experience and connections to benefit others?

- Always work to improve myself?

- Love to learn new things?

- Know how to ask for help?

- Invest in myself and my potential?

- Connect with other women in a trusting, soul-satisfying way?

- Have a positive attitude (at least 90 percent of the time!)?

- Have an awareness of my powerful impact on others?

- Dedicate myself to using my strengths, gifts and talents to make a difference in the world?

- Act in a clear, direct way with compassion and kindness?

- Appreciate, honor, credit and celebrate those who helped me along the path to my goals?

- Know (mostly!) when to say "YES!" and how to say "NO"?

- Cultivate a tough mind yet lead my life with a tender heart?

- Work toward my next desires and know that I am on my way, even if I may not yet fully know how to get there?

- Recognize my creativity as a gift to be protected, valued and nurtured?

- Give—and accept—love and support?

- Believe there is plenty in this world for me?

AN INVITATION FROM DEBBIE

I'm thrilled you found your way to us!

Right now you may be wondering what your own next steps are to being on fire with your life. As a favorite teacher of mine, Marianne Williamson, says, "Don't stop now, before the miracle happens!"

If what you've read so far and the 20 Women on Fire Aspirations speak to you, you may want to consider joining us. There are many opportunities for you to connect and thrive in the Women on Fire community.

I would be honored to have you in our ever-expanding circle! Here are a few ways to be involved:

- Become a member of Women on Fire. With membership, you will receive monthly newsletters full of inspiration, strategies, and support to help you keep your fire burning bright. You'll also receive an audio CD each month featuring an inspiring woman who will share her wisdom and more. For more information, go to www.womenonfire.com.

❀ Attend a Women on Fire tea party in your area. To be notified of events and tea parties, please join our mailing list at www.womenonfire.com.

If you are an experienced coach or facilitator and would like to learn more about starting Women on Fire tea parties or coaching groups in your area, please contact us at info@womenonfire.com.

❀ While I no longer coach women on an ongoing, individual basis, I do lead a small number of group and private Vision Days each year.

❀ Would you like to craft the next steps in your life, all while being on vacation in Paris with a dynamic, supportive group of women? For consideration in one of our celebrated group Vision Days in Paris, and to request more information and an application, please email info@womenonfire.com.

Thank you for your interest.

Here's to living a life you are on fire about!

Love,
Debbie

ABOUT
DEBBIE PHILLIPS

Debbie Phillips is the inspiring founder of Women on Fire® and a pioneer in the field of executive and life coaching. She is known for her work transforming women's lives.

In 1995, Debbie created a service for leaders and women that previously didn't exist but that she had wished for earlier in her career. Executive and life coaching were all but unheard of in her professional circles at the time, and she was among the first trained coaches in the world.

After several years of coaching individuals and teams, she founded Women on Fire in 2003 to extend the outreach of support for women's success.

Debbie also created and co-developed Vision Day,® a strategic planning day that has helped thousands of people live the lives of their dreams.

Prior to becoming a coach, she was a reporter for the *Columbus* (Ohio) *Citizen-Journal;* a deputy press secretary to former U.S. Senator John Glenn during his quest for the Democratic presidential nomination; press secretary to former Ohio Governor

Richard F. Celeste; and an executive with U.S. Health Production Co., which featured the internationally syndicated television health and lifestyle show *Life Choices with Erie Chapman.*

Debbie has a bachelor's degree in journalism from The Ohio State University and a master's degree in public administration from the John F. Kennedy School of Government at Harvard University.

She and her husband and collaborator, Rob Berkley, live with their big white cat, Wilber, on Martha's Vineyard, Massachusetts, and in Naples, Florida.

CONTACT

Debbie Phillips
Founder, Women on Fire®

Address: P.O. Box 786, West Tisbury, MA 02575
Phone: (508) 696-4949

Email: info@womenonfire.com
Website: www.womenonfire.com
Blog: www.DebbiePhillips.com
Twitter: @BeAWomanonFire and @WomanonFire
Pinterest: www.pinterest.com/beawomanonfire
Facebook: Like our Women on Fire Page. Then search Women on Fire to request entrance to our private group.
YouTube: Subscribe to receive video tips and information at www.youtube.com/beawomanonfire.

For quantity book sales or to sponsor a Women on Fire event in your area, please call (508) 696-4949.

Get the *Spark!*, your free weekly newsletter from Debbie Phillips

It's the ultimate source of life-changing ideas, important information, and announcements from Women on Fire.

Each week, you will:

→ **Find the inspiration** to move forward in your life. The spirit of Women on Fire works whether things are going well or times are tough.

→ **Connect with an uplifting community.** You'll hear about Women on Fire events taking place in your area and online.

→ **Learn strategies** to overcome the obstacles, aggravations, and confusion in your personal and professional lives.

→ **Receive support from thousands of Women on Fire.** You are not alone. We understand your needs and aspirations.

→ **Discover something** that makes you smile, laugh, or maybe cry, even as it helps you to **live the life of your dreams.**

"Although my email inbox is cluttered, I make it a date to read the Spark! from Debbie every week. It's just the nourishment I need to refuel for the week ahead."

— **Holly Getty,** New York City, fashion industry executive, personal style consultant, and co-author of Women on Fire, Volume 1.

Sign up now to get the free inspiration, strategies, and support you need for a richer, more fulfilling life, regardless of where you find yourself in that journey.

Visit www.womenonfire.com to sign up for the *Spark!* today.

www.womenonfire.com
www.debbiephillips.com
www.youtube.com/beawomanonfire
www.facebook.com/womenonfire

Become a Woman
on fire

and transform your life and career through skillful coaching and discussions with today's most inspiring luminaries. Women on Fire founder Debbie Phillips takes you behind the scenes with fascinating authors, businesspeople, spiritual leaders, artists and other professionals. Nothing is off limits as they share their struggles, journeys, and secrets for success and healing.

"The Women on Fire membership is like having a toolbox for success."

"The Women on Fire membership is like having a toolbox for success. Women On Fire is a place where you can show up looking and feeling your best, or your worst —it doesn't matter! You will always belong. The women in this community bring out the 'I think I cans' and the 'maybe I coulds' in me. As a member, I can believe in the possibility of my dreams."

*~ **Kim Dettmer,** Author/Illustrator, Berea, Ohio*

Guided by Debbie, you will have the information, inspiration, strategies and support to live a life of greater richness and fulfillment. Here are just some of the things you will receive with your monthly Women on Fire membership:

→ **A beautiful membership package** containing an audio interview, plus a transcript so you can follow along. You will be uplifted by the insightful, revealing Q&A's between Debbie and her hand-selected experts. You also receive a coaching lesson on the current topic and much more.

→ **A monthly live video chat** and coaching session conducted by Debbie.

→ **Access to the private Women on Fire Facebook page.** Get information and support as you need it from the Women on Fire community.

→ **The opportunity to participate** in the *"She's a Woman on Fire!"* feature, read by thousands of women.

→ **Your own Women on Fire membership card** with an exclusive member number that enables you to receive significant discounts and special access to members-only Women on Fire events.

Ready for something inspiring? Join the Women on Fire monthly membership now! womenonfire.com/members